THE CONDUCTOR'S WORLD

THE
CONDUCTOR'S
WORLD

D. E. INGHELBRECHT

TRANSLATED FROM THE FRENCH BY
G. PRERAUER AND S. MALCOLM KIRK

PETER   NEVILL

FIRST PUBLISHED IN 1953 BY
PETER NEVILL LTD
50 OLD BROMPTON ROAD, LONDON, S.W.7
AND 122 EAST 55TH STREET, NEW YORK

PRINTED IN GREAT BRITAIN BY
THE DITCHLING PRESS, SUSSEX

CONTENTS

This book was first published in France
under the title of *Le Chef d'Orchestre
et son équipe*

By the same Author:

COMMENT ON NE DOIT PAS INTERPRÉTER 'CARMEN', 'FAUST'
ET 'PELLÉAS'

DIABOLUS IN MUSICA. Essai sur la musique et ses interprètes

MOUVEMENT CONTRAIRE. Souvenirs d'un musicien

    I   Vers les temps heureux

   II   Vers les temps nouveaux

FOREWORD

IT is a great loss to music in this country that the name and work of Maître Inghelbrecht is not better known here. He has unselfishly subordinated his compositions to his conducting (though some readers will no doubt remember his enchanting settings of French Nursery Songs for pianoforte duet) and he has equally unselfishly neglected the career of a travelling maestro in order to devote his life to his native city, where for many years he has directed performances of the highest quality whether in the opera, the concert hall, or the wireless studio.

General readers will enjoy the skill, the wit and the charming anecdotes in the book, and conductors and conducting students will, I hope, enjoy it first and ponder over it later, for I know no book (and I have read many) which sets out the task with such competence and authority, and if it can be called a text-book, it is surely the most readable text-book ever written.

The chapter on 'Psychology' might profitably be committed to memory by any student, and under 'Technique' we may all find maxims which we can digest with profit, and make ourselves better craftsmen. Again, his hints on the length of notes, the length of rests and such things as the rhythm of the last movement of the 'Prague' Symphony are masterly and final.

I have also greatly enjoyed his dissertation on the plan of a concert hall and opera pit. Being also a diehard in this matter, I was delighted to find him arguing in favour of a balanced plan instead of the modern idea of lumping all the treble instruments on the left of the platform, and all the bass instruments on the right, thus neglecting the clear wishes of almost any composer from Mozart to the present day for antiphonal give and take between first and second violins as equal partners, whereas the plan usually adopted nowadays makes the second violins, if audible at all, simply a pale reflection of the firsts.

May I heartily commend Maître Inghelbrecht's wisdom to all those interested in conducting and the charm of his writing to all those interested in music.

May, 1953   ADRIAN BOULT

I. ENTRADA

THE first time I was asked to sit as one of the jury of the
Conservatoire competitions for student-conductors was an
illuminating experience. The tests were as follows: first, the
candidates were given a score of a work unknown to them.
They were to study it for only one hour. Then they had to
conduct it, with the orchestra sight-reading the music.
Secondly, they had to conduct the accompaniment for a
soloist. And lastly, they had to conduct a piece the orchestra
knew already. For this latter test, the Finale of Schumann's
First Symphony had been chosen. The piece to be accompanied was Saint-Saëns' *Concertstück* for violin. But for sight-
reading the director of the Conservatoire had shrewdly chosen
the most unfamiliar Liszt's symphonic poems—unfamiliar,
indeed, for the jury as well!

The competitors demonstrated all the different features
characteristic of French conductors. The first one showed that
the Prix de Rome does not of necessity confer ability to conduct upon its holder. By way of contrast, the second showed
that it is not sufficient to possess facility for gesticulating or to
have, at twenty years of age, a perfect command of platform-
manners—including a benevolent handshake for the soloist.
Knowing music and knowing how to serve it is something
altogether different. Another candidate revealed the particular
affinity which sometimes exists between conductor's baton
and violinist's bow, but also the same lack of musical depth as
his predecessor. In the end, two of the competitors were
clearly superior to their colleagues and could claim the sublime
reward due to them.

In order to judge this competition with fairness, the first
duty was to remember that we had been young once our-

A

selves, impetuous, exaggerated—and vain. That there is a stage where the budding *Kapellmeister* imagines that he is guiding his comrades, whereas in fact he does nothing else but follow them, 'miming' with his arms the music they are playing. There are even some conductors who later continue in this manner for a long, long time! Of course, the veterans sitting in judgment remarked specially on all the things which one must not do. They should have realized that even they still had something to learn. They might have asked themselves how they would have extricated themselves at their debut from a brusque encounter with Abbé Liszt's *Prometheus*, *Hungaria*, *Hamlet*, or *Mazeppa*. And the reasonable conclusion was that in our days no one ought to have the right to conduct an orchestra *unless* the necessary qualifications of a conductor are matched by a musical education 'in depth'.

The following qualifications should be compulsory for admission to the conductors' class: that a student has reached a sufficiently high stage in classes of harmony and composition, that he possesses experience of at least a string instrument, and some rudimentary knowledge of Italian and German in order to understand properly the foreign terms used in scores.

The young competitors closeted with their Liszt score only had one hour to familiarize themselves with it. Therefore none of them had the time, even if the thought had crossed his mind, to read the preamble written by Liszt in Weimar in March 1856 and meant for his interpreters of the future. He would have discovered instructions as clear and wise as those addressed by Schumann to young musicians, or by Wagner and Berlioz to conductors:

> In order to achieve a result in performance which corresponds to the intentions of my orchestral works, and in order to give them the colouring, the rhythm, the quality and the life which they need, it will be necessary to precede the general rehearsal by sectional rehearsals of the strings, the woodwind, the brass and the percussion. By this method of divided working, time will be saved while

giving the performers real knowledge of the composition. So I take the liberty of begging conductors who intend to perform one of these symphonic poems to take good care that the general rehearsals are preceded by the above-mentioned sectional rehearsals.

At the same time I must point out that in this type of composition the baton must be handled with more care, suppleness and knowledge of the effects of colouring, rhythm, and expression than has been customary hitherto in many orchestras. It is not enough to beat time during the performance and to have the work mechanically executed with more or less correctness. One cannot expect the composer to be grateful for the propagation of his work in this fashion, or to acknowledge it as a faithful interpretation of his thoughts. The vital spark of a beautiful symphonic performance lies principally in the real understanding of the performed work. In particular, the conductor must possess this understanding and also the gift of communicating it to the orchestra. He has to distribute and accentuate phrases, to indicate contrasts while smoothing out transitions. Sometimes he has to watch that the various instruments are in equilibrium. At other times, some instruments must emerge, either as isolated soloists or in groups. In some passages it is sufficient to stress certain notes or to bring them out; in others, however, it is a question of phrasing, singing, and even declaiming. It is the task of the conductor to indicate to each player the rôle he has to play.

I usually indicate my intentions concerning nuances, accelerations and *ritardandi* as clearly as possible by a detailed use of conventional signs and marks of expression. Nevertheless, it would be illusory to believe that one can put down in black and white everything that gives a performance character and beauty. The secret lies in the talent and inspiration of the conducting and playing artists alone. The amount of sympathetic understanding these artists accord to them will be the best pledge for the success of my works.

When drawing parallels between life and music, Count Keyserling said: 'A score is only a *promise* of music.' Never has a musician put the mystery and dangers of interpreting into such concise and clear words. And never was the influence of the conductor upon the orchestra, so often questioned, more clearly demonstrated than at that examination at the Conservatoire. The seven competitors, all pupils of the same teacher, had certainly had the same instruction on performing the Schumann Finale. Nevertheless, the orchestra played the piece in seven different ways. It is true that certain fundamental errors could be found with each conductor: trumpets and tympani too strong on tonics and dominants, as in all classical works; *ritardando* too early before the oboe cadenza, entry of the second horn inaccurate, and neglecting of 'con fuoco' before the cadenza of the flute . . . to a point where these traditional errors might be attributed to the teaching rather than to the pupils.

But it is impossible to utter an opinion about the teaching after just one examination at the end of the year. One would rather have to observe it while present at the lessons. It appeared nevertheless that this tuition had been purely theoretical, with the professor alone doing all the talking. However, quite a portion of practical advice given during a sort of informal conversation with them, could be infinitely more profitable for these students of conducting. Then one might really talk of work 'in depth', work, moreover, where general culture would often have to play a rôle.

There was no controversy among the jury concerning the distribution of awards, as there was naturally an inclination towards generosity rather than severity. There was only one unanimous regret: the impossibility of giving the highest award . . . to the orchestra itself! In fact, it was amazing that these apprentice players should sight-read Liszt's symphonic poems, which bristle with difficulties, with much more precision and virtuosity than the apprentice conductors had shown in conducting them. One felt a real national pride that our French orchestral school could be considered without doubt the finest in the world. In the Parliament of music, women have gained an appreciable number of seats, during recent years. In the orchestral class at the Conservatoire, the post of concert-master (leader), the solo 'cello and the majority of the string players' desks were occupied by the so-called weaker sex. And it was the 'lady tympanistes' who took it in turn to extract thunder and tempest from the copper basins in which once their ancestors had been content to cook jam for the family.

Then I remembered my old friend Philippe Gaubert who had told me that he preferred instructing future conductors rather than future orchestral players—the chair he held included both the orchestral and the conductors' courses. On the other hand, I thought that it would be far more interesting, exciting and worthwhile to prepare future orchestral players: to fashion their technique to the needs of the ensemble, to elevate their spirits above the anonymity of their task; to awaken in them a feeling of professional conscience, and to avoid already at school those old habitual mistakes, like a gardener pruning his plants and ridding them of caterpillars.

In our age of speed this would save much time for future conductors who would meet with young men better prepared for their professional task.

As I have always doubted whether it is possible to teach others to conduct an orchestra, I thought then that no young hopeful of the baton would run any risk of being led astray if the teaching was bad. I even believed that no pupil, however good a musician he might be, could acquire a 'conductor's arm' unless this gift had been granted him by nature. As if for the purpose of ironical confirmation of my belief, Gaubert's predecessors in the professorial chair, although illustrious and cultured musicians, never managed, while teaching others, to attain themselves the mastery and ease of the born conductor. By the way, what will happen to a pupil, gifted but untrained, who is guided by a teacher of this kind? Admitting that the latter had ever had the idea of talking to his pupils about the advice of Liszt, Schumann, Berlioz, and Wagner, how would they be capable of understanding what little they had been able to retain? At that moment the failure of the teacher to teach any practical knowledge, to which I have referred previously, would become obvious; so would the risk run by the willing pupil.

There should be only one way of interpreting the masters who have generally left us with sufficient indication of how to achieve it. Let us know how to read and also learn how to discover the lies of the interpolations inserted in the course of successive re-editings by revisers completely lacking in taste, culture, or scruples. At the same time, there should be only one way of conducting, the great conductors seem to be generally in agreement on this point. Because you must not confuse conducting and interpreting. . . .

Whatever similarities you may observe among the great, or simply among the *good* conductors, you will never discover servile imitation, that error from which so few beginners escape. The majority of the latter observe too superficially these models who, rather, should set them thinking for themselves. Thus many among them, once they stand in front of an orchestra, indulge specially in aping more or less skillfully some particular gestures of these models. When they watch them from the back, they have their eyes fixed on their arms alone, without noticing for example how a mere glance can convey orders. In our age of haste, young musicians no longer think of finding their best tuition by attending rehearsals of great conductors. Here alone is it possible to appreciate the real value of conductors, less by looking at them than by listening to their remarks and demands. Here, too, young composers could learn best how to orchestrate. That was what we used to do in the old days, together with Ravel, Schmitt, and so many others. We were hidden in the shadows of the halls and often chased out by the watchdogs of Colonne or Chevillard. Yet, between 1934 and 1950, more than three thousand rehearsals of the Orchestre National took place, conducted by a larger number of different conductors, without any of the young musicians deigning to attend, although they were often invited . . . and this is still going on.

Perhaps we might conclude with Paul Valéry that 'man today will not cultivate anything unless he can get it in an abridged form'. Or should we perhaps think that in certain isolated cases among young musicians there is secret discontent with the insufficiency of teaching which confines itself to one method only? And that even this method has become rather questionable because it is merely based by way of improvisation upon what 'is usually done' when conducting an orchestra?

'It is too hard for a young man stunned by war', Baudelaire would have said, 'to find himself on a rough sea without a *lighthouse*.'

It was the memory of this anguished confession in particular which induced me to compile some reflections on conducting. Repeating a formula already tested[1] and selecting from innumerable examples I have watched, I shall try to point out the most familiar and most typical mistakes made by the majority of conductors. I shall endeavour to do so without rigorous classification or pedantry, and in that haphazard manner which is the usual thing after an orchestra rehearsal when one talks over on the way home what took place. We shall proceed just in the manner of that 'round-table' teaching which I have advocated above, when in the course of friendly conversations between older and younger people some score or the other may be fetched from the library to elucidate some special point just under consideration, or for a forthcoming performance. Sometimes also we shall add to our tuition the instructions which we may have gleaned from a competent book:

> You are not serious in your intentions unless you are ready to make every sacrifice to attain your goal: otherwise, it will be simply a matter of cultivating your own ego and putting it into relief before the eyes of the world. This fallacy is spreading and

1. 'Comment on ne doit pas interprêter *Carmen*, *Faust* et *Pelléas*', by the same author (Heugel).

leads to the imitation of the modern virtuosos who do not choose those works for their repertoire which could give their audiences the greatest musical enjoyment, but rather those which can show off the brilliance of the performer.

Thus you may, during a chance reading of the *Conversations of Goethe with Eckermann*, discover these lines which apply so exactly to the person Berlioz justly called 'the most formidable intermediary between music and audience . . . '—the conductor!

II. GRAFFITI (Scribblings)

In musical performance the majority of the fundamental mistakes derive from confusing means and ends. The most common error is to mistake time for rhythm. A conductor is more inclined to make this mistake than any other interpreter. His baton risks being confined by the pitiless, mournful despotism of the metronome. The choir-master is much closer to the expressive truth of music: when beating the *rhythm* of plainsong, he will indicate the breves more discreetly than the longae, in the endeavour to preserve the phrasing which is the same for the monody and the words. It stands to reason that the same does not apply to polyphony; however, the chorusmaster in the concert hall does not conduct his singers as if they were instrumentalists. Often, influenced by the number of parts which is restricted in comparison with the number of orchestral parts, and influenced also by the verbal contents, his gestures resemble those of the (church) choir-master. When you have learned how to watch the greatest orchestral conductors, you will notice how they sometimes abandon the monotony of time-beating, and how then the meaning of their gestures increases ... until you find again in them the expressive truth of the lowly choir-master. It goes without saying that we are speaking only of the *really* great conductors —becoming, alas, less numerous every day—but not of the 'stars' of the head-tossing, rump-twisting, and cuff-shaking type. Melodic lines and even harmonic contexts will be hacked to pieces by the bar-lines and the beaten time: this the conductor ought to avoid carefully. However, the majority of them don't worry about it but generally confine their efforts to guiding their players in a tentative manner through the elementary structure of the scores.

Let us imagine a synthetic Professor Metronomus whom we will invest with all the mistakes of all their innumerable per-petrators, with all the current fashions of 'beating' music. Thus, everyone will be unable to 'guess who'. Let us go right to the centre of the subject by attacking the *graffiti* which reveal and spread the most frequent error.

Dispensing his wisdom *ex cathedra*, Metronomus will have informed his pupils that the conductor must, above all, 'pre-pare' his score. One may observe in opera houses the current usage of 'making ready' the conductor's scores, which implies a note-by-note revision of the text, undertaken by the offici-ally sworn-in copyist of the theatre. It is his task to stress by thick marks in differently-coloured pencil all the dynamics, and this down to the tiniest accents. This includes scenic re-marks, entries for the singers or for each instrument with the aid of geometrical diagrams. It includes the underlining of the words from one end of the score to the other. And, of course, the result is that all these beautiful things make a proper reading of the musical text quite unnecessary and, anyway, entirely impossible![1]

It's just the same with symphonic scores, and the multi-plicity of conventional signs which clog them reminds me a little of those transparent labels you paste on the wind-screen of learner-drivers to tell them the meaning of the road-signs.

French horn entries are preceded by a blue circle, those of the trombone, however, by a red circle ... this little salt-cellar and that masonic symbol refer to the tympani and the triangle ... whereas the optician's emblem which follows them indicates a dangerous turn-over—to the next page (where in the first bar the problematic triangle-entry threatens!)—or else the pair of glasses may indicate perhaps a brusque change of speed.

1. *Diabolus in Musica*, by Inghelbrecht: Chap. XVIII, p. 134.

When the melodic line meanders from one instrument to another, you may behold oblique lines up and down across the staves and across the bar-lines, giving the pages the appearance of a temperature chart—of the incompetence of the conductor.

Above all, Metronomus has unreservedly sworn his faith in the little instrument invented by Maëlzel which he uses quite immoderately. Scrupulously avoiding relying on his own instinct, he will always refer to a metronome-mark for a quaver or a crotchet, even if it's wrong. He has just as little confidence in his own intelligence when a *rallentando* or an *accelerando* occurs. In a passage of six to eight bars, he will mark its progress by two, three or even four marks which he will show by large, well-shaped figures. His scores make you think of account-books and he peers at them like a motorist at his speedometer.

The only addition to the text which may be useful or rather, indispensable, is the bowing. Yet this is the very thing which is generally neglected. We will come back to it later on.

The only equally justifiable addition concerns the time-signature—often hardly visible although it appears on each stave for each instrument of the score. An improvement was even tried out, without becoming generalized: the replacement of these small figures by much larger ones, printed for whole groups of instruments. However, the conductor should be able to recognize the time from the structure itself, the more so as he is supposed to have sufficiently studied the score he is going to conduct. But just here we put the finger on the wound of the majority of those who do not hesitate to conduct a score they have studied in a hurry and superficially. Hence, the greater number of hieroglyphic symbols to make a score 'fool-proof'!

These Metronomi are mostly careerists—and are essentially lazy, if they have any talent at all for the profession they have decided to follow. And they imagine—even if often quite unconsciously—that they will be able to hide their incompetence and blundering and that some good luck will extricate them. With their *graffiti* they do not underline the essential. Instead, they stress the fact that they are improvising, because time-signature and nuances are only the means. The end is the music itself, its rhythm, its notes, the chords and the contexts of chords which they form. Let us assume that Metronomus does take the time to settle down at his table for some real work at an orchestral score. Will he think of underlining a chord here and a note there which, as he begins to know and to understand the score better, he might consider necessary to put into relief? He might gradually arrive at underlining so much that he would finish by writing down every note of it again!

Performances suffer considerably from this erroneous idea of the conductor's role. Owing to the gestures which transmit them, the orchestra will reproduce the underlinings of dynamics as well as the entries and the overstressed accents in an exaggerated manner. A clever mimic, knowing nothing of music, could manage to beat time to a score quite as well as this sort of conductor, because he busies himself purely with his figures and accents, without ever caring about melodic line or harmonic progression. Hence the monotony of so many performances pieced together in this way. They give musical masterworks the unintelligibility of disorganized and roughly cemented mosaic.

Metronomus adores figures so much that there is no end to his ingenuity in applying them. Thus, in a fast Scherzo which must be conducted one-in-a-bar, he shows by sprawling marks —numbered ones, of course—sections of four, six, three, or eight bars vaguely based upon the context of phrases or phrase-fragments; and he also shows a supposed subdivision of slower bars: all this in order to 'prevent himself' from becoming confused by the persistence of the Presto. In this manner he arrives at conceiving *L'Apprenti Sorcier* as an easy

nine-eight from beginning to end, like a nice father taking
junior for a Saturday afternoon walk—although the composer
himself never gave such an indication. In fact Dukas, making
a hobby of conducting like d'Indy, Ravel and so many others
—and even of teaching conducting!—always conducting his
immortal masterpiece one-in-a-bar.

Metronomus tries to justify his weakness by quoting famous
precedents: the '*Ritmo di tre* (or, *quattro*) *battute*' in certain
passages in the Scherzo of Beethoven's Ninth Symphony, or
of Liszt's *Mephisto-Waltz*, for example. But there it is only a
question of composers having made performance easier in
their own day. The same method was used, but the other way
round, at a later date by Bizet for his chorus of cigarette-girls
in the first act of *Carmen*. The way of writing adopted by good
composers is always an adequate means for expressing their
thoughts. The rest is only a means, but not an end.

This erroneous manner of beat in fast movements generally
distorts the physiognomy of the melody, and inflates its line,
by superimposing inevitable accents on the imaginary strong
or semi-strong beats of the *supposed* slow bars. The rhythm of
the Scherzo becomes so heavy that it even loses its speed—
whereas, if beaten one-in-a-bar, the uniformity of speed does
away with the scansion of each bar, to those who understand
and respect the demands of its melodic line.

By the same kind of reasoning the multiple repetition of
one bar induces Metronomus to number successively each
repetition; no difference of musical order will ever make him
deviate from this 'preventive' measure. This may be illustrated best by looking at the *graffiti* marked on top of the last
bars preceding the beginning of the *Dies Irae* in the Finale of
the *Symphonie Fantastique*—by a conductor who enjoys fame
in Paris—which, by the way, is really well deserved for a
number of other reasons.

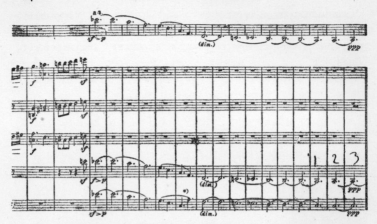

How Berlioz would have raged at the sight of this document, which staggered me no less than Weingartner when he discovered it.

Round about 1900, the editor of a musical magazine asked a number of conductors whether they thought it necessary or not to conduct from memory. If so, how would it be possible to give the correct entries in certain difficult cases, for example at the end of the Scherzo of Beethoven's Fifth Symphony. And under the title 'Entente Cordiale' he published the following two replies:

> For the famous crescendo of the C Minor Symphony I count thirteen bars before giving the entry to the second violins, and sixteen for the first violins. I do not know whether my colleagues follow the same procedure, but hitherto it has served me well. . . .
>
> CAMILLE CHEVILLARD.

> I have never found this passage difficult to conduct from memory: as far as counting bars is concerned . . . this is an expedient worthy of choral and brass-band conductors, but of which, I think, no serious musician can ever have dreamed. . . .
>
> VINCENT D'INDY.

Conducting from memory is a question we will postpone till later. As to the method recommended by Chevillard, it raises again the question of numbers, already referred to. Mnemonic or graphic signs make the conductor a prisoner of that fear of error which paralyses so many of them. And the use of the *graffiti* will result in their misuse.

For twenty years a certain pedagogue occupied the conductor's desk at the Opéra. He was the first to benefit from the confusion which the (then) director Pedro Gailhard had created. He held the Prix de Rome (a composer's prize), and he hailed from Toulouse, Pedro Gailhard's home town—but did this make him a conductor? The gentleman in question multiplied the *graffiti* in his scores. In the course of the Garden Scene of *Faust*, during the quartet, he had even marked the positions of the characters on stage, as if their costumes were not enough to distinguish them:

FAUST   MARG.   MEPHIS.   MARTHE

Nor did he forget to 'remind himself' of their change of position:

Although he was gifted with the most remarkable encyclopaedic memory, he confessed ingenuously that he never dared to take his eyes off the score, even when conducting the 'Soldiers' Chorus'! His feeling of insecurity was such that his graphic precautions became a mania. On the first page of the *William Tell* score he had written in thick blue pencil: 'Violoncello solo'! All his natural gifts had simply deserted him, and no feeling of integrity had ever told him to give up.

Integrity, no less than humility, is a virtue essential for the conductor even more than for all other interpreters. It is not

unusual for youth to be poorly endowed with it, but it is
tragic not to achieve it at a riper age. Often modesty enhances
a conductor's merit, his real merit and not that which he gets
from the untrustworthy popularity of snobs. And it is the very
greatest conductor of our time who is a living proof of this
statement.

III. TOSCANINI

MUSIC-LOVERS often find rehearsals preferable to actual performances. We have deplored in a previous chapter that young composers and conductors do not think on the same lines. When a new or a rarely played work is on the programme, it will be a great help to its understanding to hear it interrupted and partially repeated. When the conductor knows how to explain the reasons for an interruption to those in front of him, it will be useful instruction also for those hidden in the shadows of the hall.

It is obvious that too many conductors are more given to playing to the gallery behind them than to helping the players in front of them. Their imagination is unbelievably fertile and we have had to stop keeping count of the different ways in which they put into sound those 'blows of fate' of the C Minor Symphony, or in which they wallow in the love and the death of *Tristan and Isolde*, or in which they lead into battle the valiant sons of the Danube to the tune of the Rakoczy March. They speak too readily of 'their' 'Eroica', of 'their' César Franck Symphony or of 'their' *Après-midi d'un Faune*. Such musings have not the slenderest chance of success at a rehearsal where all these little clownings run the risk of rebounding on the head of the conductor given to acting in front of the orchestra as if it were a film-camera. In more ways than one the work to be done during a rehearsal for a symphony concert may be compared with a studio performance for the radio, or with the making of a gramophone record. The microphone has singularly changed the rôle of the conductor and of his players. Here the judgment of the listener remains uninfluenced by any visual impression. Conditions resemble those of the

Bayreuth performances where the orchestra and its conductor are invisible.

The listener at the rehearsal identifies himself subconsciously with the orchestral musician and shares the players' demands on the man who conducts them, when in front of him. He is pitiless concerning any ineffective gesture. He has the cruel indifference of the microphone towards the contortions of the pianist who looks as if he were just telling you in confidence: 'If you only knew how it hurts playing Beethoven with a boil in such an awkward place!'

Watching the hard work of rehearsals, you feel that there is more than one point of comparison with the patient labours of the chemist in his laboratory. Often a conductor needs much patience in order to be able to persevere until he gets the proper reaction which must emerge from a mixture of colourings or from a harmonic accumulation. It may happen that the listener is less patient in his search for precision in a passage the subtlety of which escapes him, and that he identifies himself with the majority of the instrumentalists who are generally of the opinion that 'this is near enough'! In such moments the conductor must know how to insist with great firmness, but not without diplomacy.

A phrase has not been played sufficiently *piano* for Toscanini's liking. The phrase is repeated again and again. Toscanini feels the players growing impatient. Toscanini interrupts. Suddenly he declares: 'Wait! perhaps I am wrong myself . . . all of us may be wrong sometimes . . . I'll look it up . . .'. He opens his score, leafs attentively through it, bends over it with his eyes a few inches from the staves . . . then declares, as if feeling uncomfortable at being always right: 'Oh yes! Oh yes! It is marked *pianissimo* . . .! Well, let us try again!'

Although it has often been used and abused, we may risk, with regard to the conductor, a culinary comparison: The good cook, the true, born *chef*, adds salt, pepper and spices by instinct, without any hesitation whatever. And when he tastes it—for he does taste it, he *must* taste it!—rarely must he add anything; and, of course, he will never have put in too much. Look at Toscanini, genius master-chef, before his puffing cooks and scraping scullions: he makes this note or that one stand out from a chord, he demands that this semi-quaver become less incisive and that triplet become *rounder*. He spices a ragoût with an appoggiatura and sugars the sweets with a rallentando. Looking at the grill of his score, he had told himself: 'Here . . . here . . . and there!' And his 'touch' has revealed itself immediately in a work which we thought we knew so well, like the secret aroma a *cordon bleu* of my acquaintance gives to the family stew when he adds to the customary vegetables a chubby tomato. Note also a little the mastery with which Toscanini bakes for you the pie of the *Mastersinger* prelude or thickens a sauce for you with the play of the waves in *La Mer*. . . .

It might be thought perhaps that we are mentioning subtleties which are only accessible to the élite . . . but we are not dining table d'hôte. And Toscanini, in spite of such an irreverent comparison, has not to fear discomfiture, like a certain Burgundian gourmet. . . . The latter, looking forward with pleasure to the effect he was going to produce upon his guests by their first taste of a particularly venerable Pommard, overheard one of them saying to his wife, while smacking his lips: 'I say . . . not bad at all, their little pinard!' (cheap red wine).

However, there are quite a number of lovers of an ordinary menu in the concert halls. Thus, while I was listening one day in wonderment to Toscanini rehearsing *La Mer*, I heard behind me two conductors, and not at all of a lowly rank, remark with a smile: 'Fancy telling the orchestra that he always want to hear the melody—how typically Italian!' They were quite wrong. What Toscanini asked for, was a specific *musical* issue. What he called melody, was actually the line, that thread of Ariadne which the performer must never allow the listener to lose.

Why, by the way, should Toscanini have escaped that lack of understanding which is the daily bread of the great masters? It took a long time before it was acknowledged what influence his genius could bring to bear also upon all non-Italian music. For example, I had always heard it said that Wagner was a closed secret to him. Therefore, passing through Milan, I did not miss the chance of hearing him conduct *The Mastersingers*. Is it necessary to describe the unforgettable memory of this performance. . .? 'That may be', other critics had told me, 'but never listen to him conducting Debussy. . .!' At that time, the colossal revelation of *La Mer*, one evening at the Opéra, was still a thing of the future for me.

Toscanini is beyond argument. He is the greatest conductor of our age, the equal and the successor of Nikisch and Mottl. He is a saint, an apostle, who *really is music* and lives for it. The most tremendous success does not matter to him if he himself was not satisfied by the performance! On the night of that incredible *Mastersingers* performance at La Scala, Milan, the whole theatre, rising to its feet, had just given him an ovation such as I have never heard, when he re-appeared at his desk for the last act. For almost a quarter of an hour he obstinately refused to respond. It appeared he had been dissatisfied with his oboist! More than ten years later, reminding him of this evening, he was told how his indifference had really pained those who loved him and shouted their admiration for him. Then he answered, with his attractive lisp: 'But think just for a moment, I simply couldn't, it was quite impossible: that oboe had hurt me so terribly!'

Even from the simple point of view of mere physique his case is incomprehensible. Some time before his arrival in Paris, a tendentious campaign had been started by one of our critics against conductors who make so many gestures that their shirt-collars become saturated with perspiration. Simply a question of fashion and of publicity, he said. What should one then think about Toscanini whose constant expenditure of energy is almost superhuman and who soaks not only his collar but also his shirt, his waistcoat and even his coat to such an extent that he has to have a complete change at each interval? 'It is like that', he said to me simply. 'I have only to conduct the overture of the *Barber* for it to happen!' He never spares himself. And yet he seems as if he could stay on for twice or three times as long as a concert lasts, stalking about the edge of the platform without weakening for a moment, simply because he has willed it so.

Hardly has he left the orchestra, dripping even more with perspiration after a rehearsal than after a concert, his voice husky from continual comment and explanation, he will still talk of music as he moves away. If anything could be more striking than his unequalled mastery of conducting and his prodigious memory, it would be this constant fervour of his. It explains and justifies his demands, his intransigence and rudeness on the platform. A cor anglais insufficiently expressive, a clash of cymbals which misfires, and he will break his baton in two. He knows, of course, that an orchestra will not go all out at rehearsals, giving its best only when in front of the public, like the majority of conductors. So he harasses them. *He* would *never* do that—spare himself! 'You always do things *one-half*...! Don't play *as if it were a habit*...!' How could anyone resist that left hand of the former 'cellist, the sublime *vibrato* of the second finger on his heart which must surely extract the last bit of feeling from the players, in one unique expressive surge?

In the same manner, Toscanini enforces his will upon us and makes us accept a most unforeseen treatment of a familiar work. The first movement of the César Franck Symphony he takes rather slower than usual, and once more we surrender to its charm. The second movement, generally taken too slow, pleases us better in the unexpected scherzo-character he gives it. There is a similar surprise in the Scherzo of Beethoven's Seventh, especially in the Trio to which he gives the speed of a Viennese waltz, whereas it is usually taken too slow, strangely enough by the Germans who, we have to say quite plainly, take more questionable liberties with their classics than anyone else.

Under Toscanini, we find that Beethoven's generally too-prominent brass—'the metal', as they say in Spain—becomes more temperate. It generally thunders indiscreet tonics and dominants. He treats it in the same manner elsewhere, in Wagner as well as in *La Mer*. The brass, under Toscanini, always remains a part of the orchestra. It does not 'detach itself from the others' in obedience to the left fist which some 'conductors' brandish.

Invited by the State Radio, Toscanini agreed to come and conduct two concerts at the Opéra, thus conferring upon the young Orchestre Nationale its greatest honour. In the interval of the first rehearsal, the great conductor said to a friend: 'You can't imagine what I feel like when I have my first rehearsal with an orchestra'. 'Indeed', said the friend, 'you must often get tired of having to deal with new players all the time, players you don't know, and whom you have to tell all over again what you had to tell so many others in the past.' 'No! no!' Toscanini interrupted. 'I have just the same feelings when I go back to my own orchestra: I feel always as if I had to pass an examination all over again!' And this is so true! How many conductors are aware that, once they mount the rostrum, the orchestra is their stern and learned jury?

After the rehearsal, Toscanini was asked whether he had read his biography by the German musical writer, Paul Stefan. 'I have tried to read some lines of Stefan Zweig's foreword', he replied, 'but you really must believe me when I tell you that I am far too modest to read what is written about me!'

This man, who might create among all true believers in the

religion of music the impression that he is a saint, could also give all those who dare to appear before an orchestra the gravest lesson in humility. He possesses a shyness and reticence which is only rarely mentioned when people discuss his personality.

You have only to hear him rehearse the Funeral March from *The Twilight of the Gods* to become aware that, whatever you may have thought yourself, it is mostly he who is right. And if he is right, it is because he does not add anything of himself and because he endeavours purely—and with what tenacity—to force his whole orchestra to play this slow piece simply *in time*, in its own, correct, slow time—this piece which is so infinitely difficult through its fluctuations and its counterpoint of ternary and binary rhythm. So long as he does not achieve the same tone-value for the two harsh chords at the beginning, he will persevere. He will explain that they had been wrong in *always* playing the second chord of the first beat and the chord preceding the third beat less strong. Then he will proceed to the fourth beat of the *same* bar, dwelling on the chromatic triplet-figure of the basses, which he will take neatly to pieces, because it is being hurried, and this always and everywhere, in the attempt of somehow patching it up. 'I have given this triplet lesson in vain all over the world', he says. He might be dealing with the *Siegfried* motif or with that of the sword—he always insists on *every tone* being played by the brass without 'letting the sound go' afterwards, but being maintained with an absolute tenuto. For the musicians present at this rehearsal this page of Wagner, so concentrated and therefore perhaps one of the summits of his work, sounded clearer than ever before. You no longer imagined the disguised supers of the Opéra clumsily starting to march behind a litter of sterilized greenery on which lay a plumpish Siegfried. You saw the massive conquerors of the Walsungs in their tragic funeral march approaching with heavy steps the *Halle* where the race of the Gods must destroy themselves.

Toscanini, who had given us the revelation of *La Mer*, was also to bring us that of the *Nocturnes*. Rarely could the balance of the first piece have reached such a perfection. He had told the orchestra: 'This morning we have played the notes, now let us play the music. . . . I don't want to feel that here are clarinets and there bassoons. I want to close my eyes and see clouds. . . .' And we really did see them with him. In *Fêtes* there was no need to be afraid he would add that absurd hold-up, traditional and spectacular, before the mysterious funeral procession. We were not accustomed to hearing it pass so quickly on its way. But it became all the more irresistible from the fact that it justified precisely the half-speed of the initial movement, especially at its recapitulation.[1] How could we help being swept off our feet by this visionary of sounds who even divined, without knowing about them, the majority of Debussy's instrumental modifications which were to be published in the re-edition of the work?

In the case of the *Danse Macabre*, on the other hand, it is the slowness which surprises us first. Therefore, Toscanini usually reassured his friends in advance by telling them this story: 'Once, during a rehearsal in Italy, one of his old conductor colleagues had hinted to him timidly: "You know, Toscanini, I simply cannot help telling you, this should be played faster." However, Saint-Saëns, who came a little later, was to confirm the maestro's idea. Even before he heard the work, he cordially took Toscanini by the shoulders and said to him: "Above all, not too fast! Just the speed of a moderate waltz!" '

Through his performance of this rather hackneyed old symphonic poem Toscanini showed us in a most startling fashion his genius for putting things right. Hitherto, we had never been quite able to discover the secret of the *Danse Macabre*, simply because we had never played it at the exact speed.

The *Benvenuto Cellini* overture had never been brought to

1. We shall return to this passage from *Fêtes* in the chapter on Technique.

life with such a breath of romanticism. Towards the end he
desired, demanded and obtained from the orchestra even more
power for this supreme and violent effort. He had told the
strings, pointing at the brass: 'It is against these gentlemen that
you have to fight!' And the strings succeeded in valiantly
holding their own and in achieving their triumph.

By including in his first programme Cherubini's Symphony
in D Toscanini gave us a surprise. But he only had to remind
us that Sarette, the founder of the Conservatoire, had said of
the Florentine, the second director of that glorious school, that
'he had stood by France in difficult times', and had cheerfully
delegated his authority, to him.

The most touching event during one of Toscanini's spring
visits to France was, for those who loved and honoured this
greatest conductor, the celebration of the fiftieth anniversary
of the day in June when he had stood for the first time on the
conductor's rostrum.

Nineteen years old, he was engaged as 'cellist in a Rio de
Janeiro orchestra when he was unexpectedly called upon by
his colleagues to save the desperate situation which had arisen
through the non-appearance of the conductor.

One cannot repeat too often how Toscanini towers miraculously over everyone—not only over the best conductors of
our time, but probably over even the most illustrious of the
past.

The manifestation of this genius should give us confidence
in the survival of the work of the interpreter, through the
example he has left for those who know how to observe and
understand. At the same time it must be repeated that even
Toscanini has not escaped being misunderstood. An excellent
instrumentalist of the Paris orchestra which Toscanini conducted, coldly said to someone who was enthusing about him:
'Yes, he's very polished—but no one could work like that all
the time!' Another, delighted at having at last discovered at a
rehearsal a slight oversight of the maestro, confided to his

neighbours: 'There, you see . . . just like the others! . . . Hə isn't really serious! . . . .' Doesn't this *sancta simplicitas* sufficiently confirm the fact that some orchestral players, generally quite able to distinguish between good and bad conductors, have no means of recognizing a *great* one among those that are just good?

Among the audience which he tolerates so good-naturedly in his rehearsals, how many 'experts' mockingly comment on his movements, his reprimands, or his entreaties? They still don't understand that independently of his prodigious gifts of musicianship and virtuosity, of his miraculous memory which absolutely compensates for his near-blindness, Toscanini possesses to the highest degree the essential virtue of the conductor: that of 'knowing what to demand'. It was a writer who showed the best comprehension of this. The admirable foreword by Stefan Zweig to the book by Paul Stefan demonstrates that no musician had ever succeeded in analysing the miracle of Toscanini deeply enough or in explaining it with as much clarity.

We know by now very many anecdotes of the terrifying demands of this magician of the orchestra. Even in his youth, no ambition to get on would ever have induced him to make the slightest concession concerning the number of rehearsals he deemed indispensable. In his early days, when he had to conduct at a small Italian town, he demanded one more rehearsal, as the standards of the performance did not yet satisfy him. The rehearsal was refused. 'Very well, I'll go!' he declares. Immediately he sets off for the station. But there he discovers he is penniless—impossible to take the train. And calmly he decides to return home on foot, and begins his walk. It would have taken him three days. But the management of the theatre had changed its mind. Everywhere they look for Toscanini. Later they find him, on the road out of town. He goes back to the theatre: at last he has the rehearsal he had demanded. In the fiftieth year of his career he declared at one of the rehearsals for the last concert in Paris: 'The best orchestra plays badly if it has not rehearsed enough'.

However, the Toscanini concerts of that particular Paris season coincided with other festive events which failed to correspond to his ideas. Other foreign conductors had consented to give at the Opéra performances of *The Mastersingers*, of *Fidelio*, and of *Don Giovanni* and to have only two rehearsals of each work. Would the conductors have agreed to this in Berlin or Salzburg? Or would the Berlin or Salzburg managements have agreed to it? If it is true that Toscanini did not fail to give the two offenders a piece of his mind, he was quite right! The visitors were two *Kapellmeister* whose value was highly appreciated in France. Thus, what they ought to have demanded was more and more time to explain to orchestra and chorus their ideas 'in depth' of the masterworks of Mozart, Beethoven, and Wagner. But the most they could do in the allotted two rehearsals was but to scratch the surface of the 'French way' of playing them. The orchestra of our Opéra can rival the world's best and deserves to be given the chance of doing so—by simply being allowed the *time* to work, with conductors worthy of the players. But it is we who ought to insist. Quite a number of foreign conductors seem to think that their mere presence at the desk suffices to *raise* the standards of an operatic or concert performance in Paris. So they neglect to take the necessary trouble to deserve the hospitality which we so lavishly extend to them.

If orchestral players often rebel against discipline because they don't always understand its real strength and nobility, we must also remember that most conductors are themselves unready to submit to that discipline which they expect from their subordinates. Some conductors have through long practice specialized in a limited repertoire and can be relied upon to interpret it with definite perfection. They are no longer concerned with anything except reducing their personal effort during rehearsals, in order to 'spare themselves' for the performances.

Others have decided, once and for all, upon the passages which they are going to interrupt, and upon the remarks—or the shafts of wit—they are going to hurl at the orchestra. One of the latter gentry never failed to say at a certain passage of *L'Après-midi d'un Faune* depicting by his words the dalliance of the goat-footed satyr: 'With his backside in the grass!' How great was his embarrassment when one day, the very moment he stopped, the whole orchestra roared out the familiar joke he was just going to utter!

This type is oblivious of the real nature of a conductor's job. He thinks he has done a satisfactory day's work when he himself gets through such-and-such a score, when he himself gets to the end of a professional performance. It never occurs to him that he might improve on his achievement, nor that the eternal 'begin again' of the conductor's task always demands of him that he shall take still the same pains with the same work—tomorrow as yesterday.

Let us get back to Toscanini, still spending his energy, never counting the cost, in the fiftieth year of his career. Although he has performed it already a thousand times with greatest glory—writes Stefan Zweig—his work remains for him at the same time a joy and agony. As a contrast, let us remember the last deceptive appearance of Richard Strauss at the desk in Paris, for a mournful performance of his works. He had had no compunction in leaving the hasty preparation to a deputy. The conclusion is clear: only a Toscanini never finishes his task. Nor does he 'begin again'—he 'continues'.

It is unusual for conductors to preserve in their days of glory a flair for prospecting for new works. Even among the great of the past, none would agree to depart often from the 'repertoire' they had built up. Apparently in vain had the founders of the *Société Musicale Indépendante* once suggested to Nikisch to conduct the first performance of Florent Schmitt's

Psaume. Like most of the great soloists, the orchestral *stars*, as Stravinsky called them, are only too ready to believe that their name is sufficient to create interest in a programme consisting of items particularly suitable to their own style.

Toscanini, on the contrary, takes advantage of his world-wide success to force the audience to listen to unknown works the choice of which sometimes even bewilders the players. The reasons for this choice may often be found in his sense of justice, of logic, or of kindness.

Every time this greatest of conductors revisited France, he had a new lesson to teach us, of honesty and of perseverance. One lesson was to remind those who conduct that they can never demand enough of themselves or of others. 'In life', he proclaims, 'we need democracy. But in art we need aristocracy.' He had just held forth on his disgust at the disgraceful habit of some players who save up all their efforts for the performances. He, Toscanini, never spares himself! He threw his score down with a burst of anger which caused a grumbling in the orchestra. But this did not make him feel put out. Far from it. He did not leave the instrumentalists with any illusion concerning his own attitude in the future, but roared: 'And I'll always behave like this!' Another time after long attempts at getting what he wanted by persuasion, and not having been very successful, he calmly closed his score and said: 'It isn't what I wanted. I did not enjoy it, but my conscience is easy.' All the same, at the end of a concert, or even after a good rehearsal, the master would wipe out all traces of ill-feeling with a gesture of satisfaction. He made such demands on our French musicians because he knew and appreciated their value. It has been said and justly deplored that the snobs—rather late in the day—took up Toscanini to such an extent that he got sick of seeing them crowd his concerts. At last they even began to find out that it was the right thing to be seen at his rehearsals. This was unbearable, because they forgot all discretion and became a nuisance to the intimate professional

circle which had gathered to hear the teaching of the supreme
master.

IV. COMMEDIANTE

IN the second chapter we have tried to summarize all that might be taught by Professor Metronomus. Now let us try to make another imaginary synthesis of another sort of *bâtonneurs* who could be described so well by Pope Pius VII's celebrated dictum referring to Napoleon.

In Chabrier's adorable *Education manquée*, the young and chaste Gontran who has just married his cousin Hélène blames his pedantic tutor for having taught him everything, in fact, too much . . . except the very essentials which he still does not know, a few moments before his wedding night! The tutor, in a funny duet, harps on all the -ics and -isms he has taught his pupil, and the ingenuous husband complains in exasperation:

'That's all very well, Pausanias! But it isn't enough!'

In contrast to the arithmetics, the dialectics and the mechanics of Metronomus, Il Maestro Commediante will preach to his flock from the same pulpit the convincing and suggestive virtues of his plasticity and his mimings, of his dynamics and gymnastics, of his ditherings, twistings and contortions, of his tremblings, and his stamping, his frisking, his prancing and jigging. We have spoken about it before,[1] but this quite inexhaustible subject is worth mentioning again.

'Above all, you must be wealthy!' Commediante will leave no doubt at all on this point at the beginning of his course—a career of this kind is inaccessible to the needy.

There must be no misunderstanding about this: these mountebanks of music must not be confused with sincere artists who sometimes can and even do spend their wealth liberally for the realization of an ideal. Neither Colonne nor

1. *Diabolus in Musica*, chapters IV, VI, IX, XV, XVIII, XXV.

Lamoureux could have existed without private means, and Pasdeloup, that forerunner of great French conductors, had to abandon his bold attempt because of lack of finance. And if his name still means something in French professional circles, it is simply because a clever *entrepreneur* had the idea of buying it up from needy heirs almost fifty years after his death. The names of Colonne and Lamoureux, however, continue to be closely connected with the work initiated by themselves.

But if they had not had money of their own, these two great conductors would still have been appointed to the Opéra orchestra, whereas Il Commediante, without money, would never succeed in appearing on the lowliest rostrum. Sometimes he knows almost nothing about music, and he often lacks the essentials necessary for a conductor. If one relies on the verdict of the orchestral players, those who have known Colonne and Lamoureux will say that they were real conductors! Whereas even those who benefited directly from Il Commediante's munificence will still proclaim that he isn't a conductor at all . . . but a clown! And there will be no end of stories of his incompetence and blunders. The following is a true story brought back from America by one of our best Parisian clarinettists: a certain Komediansky who had succeeded in getting himself appointed as head of a lush Philharmonic in the U.S.A., after having spent a lot of money in vain in an attempt to get taken on in Paris, always eluded all questions concerning harmony which were put to him at rehearsals. The result was that the musicians amused themselves by embarrassing him with asking just this sort of question. One day our clarinettist asked him whether some E or B should be a flat or a natural. The conductor, troubled and at bay, replied: 'Oh! I beg you, monsieur, let's make music and not interrupt all the time!'

Let us return to the imaginary teachings of our pedagogue which our digression interrupted just now: '. . . Well then, now that we have established that you are rich, buy yourself a pick-up, a choice gramophone library, and a good-sized mirror. Attend many concerts. *See* how others conduct, and when a gesture or an attitude appeals to you, and you think it is worth adopting, go home, try it over for yourself in front of your mirror to the accompaniment of your gramophone. After several years of patient research, hire yourself an orchestra, and pick a good one for preference. It should be easy, for you can always find among old instrumentalists some jack-of-all-trades who will be ready to aid a wealthy conductor. One of them will soon become your factotum, and then it won't be long before you are giving your first concert. It is only the first step which costs money—very much money, of course! So don't be stingy with publicity. Boldly demand that "knowing you" must take place of "your knowing"! In due course you will see the day when you get your expenses back. . . .'

If it is hardly important for the conductor of normal ability whether he is tall or short, paunchy or slim, or whether he wears his hair long or short, this certainly does not apply to our Commediante whose success is closely connected with his physical attributes. He must have a slender figure and he must dress elegantly. Short arms will be a handicap, but pale, fine, long hands an advantage. His hair must be abundant and easily ruffled rather than smoothed down; a rebellious curl which drops over the eye is excellent, just like the dishevelled and dripping mop of a boxer in the decisive round! . . .

A boxer, indeed. . . . Because this conception of the art of conducting draws less on music than on sports, not only on boxing but also on fencing, swimming, and tennis. Familiar with the tennis court, for instance, Il Commediante sometimes applies its technique to the orchestra. With a twist of the body he will reply with a back-hand to a ball from the tympanist which he will return with an astute feint to the trombones. When—during a quiet set—he allows himself the 'phoney routine' of conducting 'from memory', he seems to throw to

C

his partners a good-humoured: 'Go on, boys!', which rather means: 'I'll follow you!'

For since the miracle of Toscanini, prowess of memory has become one of the most sought after achievements. A certain star conductor from across the Alps, invited to conduct a Paris orchestra, tried to dazzle his hosts with a display worthy of Inaudi. One of the players tells this story: 'You know Fausta, the mind-reader down in the amusement-park, who has her eyes blindfolded and is asked by her stooge: "What do you see?"—"A watch."—"What metal?"—"Gold."—"What number inside the watch?"—"25,042." Well, our maestro used almost the same method with the orchestra. Addressing the trombone, he said imperiously: "What have you on page 3, line 11, bar 3, second beat?"—"It's a B!"—"What B?"—"B flat!"—"What value?"—"A quaver."—"What quaver?"—"Dotted."—"That dot is a mistake—it's a fault in the paper and the rest has been omitted by the printer!" And so forth. . . . And the players will think, like the character in *L'Education manquée*:

'That's all very well, Commediante! But it isn't enough!'

All over the world you find him—Commediante is a cosmopolitan . . . and the various breeds of this chicken-brained biped are innumerable. For, just as the public with its snobbery and ignorance mistakes him for a real musician, some of the latter debase themselves quite often by employing his recipe in order to achieve facile success.

It also occurs that Commediante meets Metronomous in the same confusion of means and ends, and of causes and effects. Hence that exaggeration of nuances and accents which often renders performances unbearable, more especially of classical works. Hence also that mania for giving beats in silent bars, for subdividing sustained tones, and for 'depicting', as if knitting, with the end of the baton the melody, or even the music played by a soloist.

Commediante loses some of his dignity when he finds himself no longer in front of *his* orchestra which is used to *his* monkey-tricks. Making an appearance with another orchestra, he will become worried, nervous, touchy, and even sometimes aggressive—the more so if the musicians of the other orchestra maintain a calm and attentive dignity. Pierné, who was pitiless where these platform cheats are concerned, used to claim even that they could only 'debunk themselves' before a mediocre orchestra. 'Nothing bad can happen to them with our great orchestras', he said, 'whereas the appearance of one of those clowns in front of a bad orchestra would be like X (a celebrity of the piano whose weaknesses as a man and artist Pierné detested) playing on a seaside concert-party piano!'

But when struggling with the score of a work new to him, our jester has no leisure any more for strutting for the gallery's benefit. Abandoning his contortions he will then be forced to stick to conducting . . . or at least to following the orchestra with his beat!

Is it perhaps jazz which has emboldened Commediante? Then he didn't understand its lessons: for Jack Hylton's comic sketches have laid bare the inanity of the lyrical or blustering attitudinizing of the conductor. Nor was the lesson always understood, by the way, by those who have adapted jazz to the Continent and more particularly to France. The *boys'* subtle and sharp Anglo-American sense of humour has nothing in common with the cheap jokes of our jazzband-suburbanism. As far as certain *ersatz* of their music is concerned, their *hot* or their *swing*, it makes me think too often of the old Saint-Saëns anecdote: he was invited to listen to a child who was supposed to 'perform brilliantly' at the piano. After hearing the child, the master crossed the family drawing-room in silence, shut the instrument, putting the key in his pocket; then, before he went out, he patted the culprit on the cheek and said, 'Noisy little fellow!'

In a type of illustrated magazine which one only finds now in a doctor's or a dentist's waiting-room, you can see in retrospect what was once the fashion of the day. Thus I found a double-page of one of them devoted to 'The Eloquence of the Hands'... of a conductor. There was a brief blurb, and I was able to learn that only the interest aroused by the sketches of Rembrandt, Franz Hals, Dürer or Rodin was comparable to the value of eight photos with evocative titles: 'Music sweet and graceful'—'Very delicate and capricious'—'The violins must sing'—'With great tension'—'Great espressivo'—'A hard, dramatic accent'—'Mighty and noble'—'Calming down'. As for the hands themselves, they simply repeated the more or less expedient gestures which most time-beaters feel obliged to make, and which have more effect on the public than on the orchestra. Not, of course, on that portion of the public which comes to listen, but on the others who go as they would to a music-hall, to see a juggler or a conjurer—with whom the magazine-commentator ingenuously compared his conductor.

I also remembered the graffiti once discovered by Chevillard in a score: 'one step to the left ... straighten up ... from behind the head (?) ... threatens the trombones'—the latter phrase might have served just as well as a title for the outstretched fist of 'A hard, dramatic accent'. It reminded me also of a young beginner who once told me in confidence how a teacher-Commediante had amused him by referring to what he chose to call the 'Work of Stage-Producing': 'Harass the violins with your left hand ... this yields another gesture for you!'—a word which could have illustrated the phrase 'The violins must sing'!

Then I remembered the time of my youth when I played the violin or viola at the Concerts Rouge, a curious little place, long since gone, on the left bank of the Seine. In the centre of the tiny hall with its low ceiling was a platform with forty musicians. The leader-conductor was a long-haired and bearded 'cellist, the absolute personification of all those 'artists' who, according to popular imagination, populate

Montmartre and the Quartier-Latin. In order to give us entries, the conductor held his bow high up in the air like a sabre,
then brought it down on the strings of his instrument (he
treated them much too roughly). His musicians put up with his
fantastic gestures, except for the drummer Larruel, a Parisian
celebrity of that period who could not stand the peremptory
gestures aimed at him by the imperious bow. One day he burst
out: 'I'll always come in on time, you can be sure of that—but
only under one condition: that you leave me alone. If ever
again you give me an entry, I'll make my exit!'

How many players of today would have to make their exit
from the orchestras if they were still as punctilious! In those
days they had also other ways of showing their displeasure. It
is known that some of them once declared to a bad conductor
who tried to make them responsible for a bad performance:
'If you say that again, next time we'll play as you conduct, and
you'll see where you are!'

It is generally ignored or forgotten that a good orchestra is
able to save the worst, as well as spoil the performance of the
best conductor. The mediocre conductor may succeed in
being taken for 'good' purely by 'bluff', in the large cities and
especially in Paris where the quality of instrumentalists is
generally excellent and where the most extensive repertoire is
known to all of them. In the orchestral world as in politics—
and often by the latter's intrusion into art—how many conductors are there who think they are leading the playing while
in reality they are being led by the players?

Before a pianist, violinist or 'cellist appears on the platform,
he must have done a little more than practise his scales and
other exercises. But a baton and a handful of willing musicians
are sufficient to make a sorcerer's apprentice believe that he is
as capable of unleashing the elements as his master. Therefore
so many who were failures as instrumentalists or composers
have no compunction in setting themselves up as conductors,
enjoying a security from punishment of a kind unavailable to

any other performer. Similarly, certain deserters from the other professions, hitherto simply amateur-musicians, sometimes decide to turn professionals, convinced like Molière's *Précieuses* that 'people of quality know everything without ever having learned it'.

One becomes conscious of the situation in an epoch like ours. The storm-troubled waters take a long time to recover their clarity, and whoever succeeds in riding out the gale is not necessarily always the purest. In music as everywhere else, we find that real values have been outclassed by a sort of inflation. There were never so many examples of this, and it lowers our prestige in the eyes of other countries. The symphonic societies and similar organizations ought to be more concerned about it.

It is not at all futile to pause and examine the case of the most obnoxious parasite of music, for his example has too often become contagious to real musicians well on the way to serving their art with dignity. It is a pity that those who are *able* to do so much want to do so little and, succumbing to the temptation of easy success, have no other desire but to sell their talents to the highest bidder. Thus there are many cases when it would be impossible to say that Il Commediante does not love music. But he loves it in his own fashion. He loves it for his own sake, but not for music's.

In the retrospective survey of my dentist's magazines I also found criticisms of *Fantasia*, Walt Disney's film. The musical accusations made against *Fantasia* assumed the character of a charge against the conductor who had collaborated in the enterprise. It was not the question of an obscure nobody of the films, or of a studio-specialist less concerned with music than with business. But it was the case of a famous *conductor*.

Just as we deplore in France the tendency to favour the cynicism of mediocrities, it might also be deplored that, in the country of the dollar, people tolerate any licence from celebrities. But what we have taken exception to, in the above lines, is really quite irrelevant—at least according to one of the critiques which assured us that Mr Stokowsky was treated in America as public enemy No. 1—just as much for having appeared on the screen as a devil of the Chatelet as for having reduced the 'Pastoral' Symphony to a quarter of an hour.

There would have been more honest attraction and even a certain educational value in a film showing the work of an orchestra and its conductor. Attempts of this sort have been made, more or less successfully. But *Fantasia* managed to surpass in mediocrity the French *Carmen*, *Louise*, and *Arlésienne* attempts.

Those whom nature has endowed with particular talents should leave to those without, the expedient of threatening the trombones and harassing the violins. They ought to consider that however vain their gesticulations may be, the musicians in the orchestra do sometimes look at them . . . and judge them, too!

V. ANALOGIES

THE task of the conductor is comparable to that of the surgeon. The score on the desk is as defenceless as the patient on the operating table. It is as if the same anaesthetic prevented both full score and patient from reacting against lack of skill, mistake, or carelessness of operators. The pages, like the body, are one entity which must first be cut open, taken to pieces, reduced to chaos, before being resuscitated.

No one would expect a surgeon to take less care at his one-hundredth appendectomy, but one often puts up with the nonchalant operation of the Doktor-Kapellmeister at his one-hundredth 'Eroica'. Even for the simplest operation a surgeon will always take care that the attention of his assistants and his nurses never relaxes and that they remain alert and increase their proficiency with each repeated operation—whereas most of our orchestral conductors seem still to live in Molière's age and, with regard to sterilization, still at the barber-leech era! The problem of the monotony of doing the same job over and over again is solved by the surgeon. By dint of operating again and again for the same complaint, he often succeeds in discovering some operating or therapeutic improvement. It is by frequent repetition of the same works that a conductor has it in his hands to discover a new secret which will serve him also with all other works.

Like Art, Science has its false priests. In medicine those who profit from illness have often been denounced, grafting being a commercial rather than a surgical operation. When one has suffered from grafting in one's own profession, one is bound to arrive at a cruel scepticism concerning current practices in Art and Science. But not everything is as hopeless as it seems. If we look closely at the medical world, at everything that belongs to it, at the beehive of a hospital, we shall probably find as anywhere else the typical French surface of irony and humbug which so often irritates and worries us. It is the same as in the orchestra where the solo 'cellist or the flautist may make a jest while conscientiously fulfilling his task. The nurse will inform the assistant that she is glad it isn't her turn to have her stomach cut open ... without thinking that the anaesthetic has not yet fully annihilated the patient's auditory faculties. But when he is at last completely unconscious at the end of the *decrescendo* of an anaesthetic which delivers him into the surgeon's hands, the miracle of organization will happen around him and for his benefit. Just as the conductor works, fights and ultimately triumphs over matter and the inert force of the orchestra, despite the difference of purpose in its components which he has come to tame and to subject to his own will, so will the surgeon compel the different components and blind forces of the organism of the body to rearrange themselves in order henceforth to follow the new directions he has just given them! And those around the master, the assistants and nurses, gaze in admiration at the building up of the *crescendo* which is to lead the patient back from the confines of oblivion to the light, by sure and steady progress.

Evidently we are not yet accustomed to taking the execution of our duties to music as seriously as all this ... because there is no comparison between the risks of a spoiled performance and of a spoiled operation. One might add that we have seldom the luck of 'operating' in a quiet, neat and tidy hospital which would reassure us concerning the proper care required for saving Schumann's *Faust*, or *La Damoiselle Elue*. But there is one additional factor: there is a state of mind still in existence among doctors which, among musicians, has completely vanished.

When Paul Funck-Brentano was complimented on his mastery, after a very grave but successful operation which, great practician that he was, he had performed with ease and speed without haste, the famous surgeon simply answered: 'Believe me, if I am successful, I owe it purely to the teaching of my master Gosset'. And in Professor Gosset's book, *Chirurgie-Chirurgiens*, we find the same respect for his own masters. Doctors still believe in the 'cult' of the teacher, of the *Master*, without blindly following his theories, but rather his trend of thinking which will lead them on the path to new discoveries.

Our young musicians are busy wheedling themselves into 'contacts' when they would be better occupied with wheedling themselves into their degrees. How then can they be expected to 'remember' a 'master'? And a master, at that, whom they may not have known too well because they may not have attended his lectures often enough? And yet it is one of the forms of idealism to preserve the cult of a master.

We have to admit that the problems of our age have more and more forced those who ought to live for music to live *by* it—but there is also another reason: the total absence of professional planning for youth. If we assume that it is normal to choose a child's career, it is certainly abnormal to force him to go on with it unless he reveals his talent at an early stage. No one seems ever to have thought of applying the principles of horticulture to general culture. Nevertheless, art and science may gain by pruning, thinning out, and by the suppression of parasite outcrops! How many of the latter choke our profession, how many 'gluttons' gorge themselves with sap at the expense of the neglected, 'healthy shoots'! Never was there as much need as today for the really keen youngster to feel that he is 'discovered', appreciated, encouraged, and helped by those who had been themselves the successful 'youngsters' of a bygone happier period.

Just like the surgeon, the conductor has his assistants—deputy-conductors, chorus-masters, and répétiteurs whom we ought to call, as at Bayreuth, 'musical assistants'. Very few would be entitled to this noble claim. We have to think of this minority of the few. Extremely conscientious in the accomplishment of their tasks, these exceptional people, too, pass silent judgment on the conductors they serve. Because they know so well 'how not to conduct', they deserve a mention here as contrasting with the Commedianti and Metronomi whom they mercilessly criticise.

'I shall never get used to working with the deaf', one of them wrote me.

'I am so pleased to hear you are writing this book. Don't forget to shoot down those hacks who change our masterworks into stuffed dummies under the pretext of exactitude. Nor need I tell you which of the masterworks come from our studios like guinea-pigs from a laboratory.

'What horrifies me most is that one or another score is now being "discovered" as a masterpiece: "I'll tell you, every unknown work *I* deign to conduct, you will see, becomes *ipso facto* the great new discovery of tomorrow"!'

Yes, it is utterly appalling, all those people who love music so much when music loves them so little. They are fully aware of it, and one might say that they only dare to pick music up with a pair of tweezers. But it comes out of their grip (it simply has to be said) greasy, or stuffy, or as a monstrosity! But it really isn't their fault because doubt-less no one has ever told them that 'to have music within oneself is the one thing that cannot be learned'.

However much one may have a taste for quotations, one often is afraid of satisfying it. At the beginning of his book, Professor Gosset says that he was afraid of adorning his lectures with quotations until one day he found these lines in Emerson:

The choice of a quotation reflects honour on the person who makes it. Those who quote confer more glory than they receive help. If another's words express what you want to say, use them as liberally as you would the language itself or the alphabet which does nothing to detract from your originality.

Is not the quotation, in fact, like a confession 'for those who have no liking for criticizing but who prefer to feel the enjoyment of admiring'? How could we resist quoting Professor Gosset in his turn, when some of his remarks might so well have been addressed to musicians!

He tells us that once, having installed himself in a cheap room, all he had in this world was five hundred francs. And he adds: 'I was privileged, for my master, Terrier, had only twenty! The young generation who see their masters only when they have succeeded, cannot understand that all of them have had difficult beginnings and that success demands plenty of hard work.' Those who were young at that time would never have become masters if they had not been determined to work hard. And efforts our young people of today must make, in order to become in turn the masters of tomorrow.

'Heroism only begins when a certain inner resistance has been conquered; only when man asks more of himself than he can achieve with ease.' This is André Gide, who continues, talking of his youth:

> We who belonged to Mallarmé's circle, were ashamed of the idea of making money by literature. To be paid meant, for us, to sell oneself—in the worst meaning of the word. It was the time when Barres, going into politics, seemed to us to have abdicated, to have fallen from his pedestal.

Politics are now a current short cut to success which artists have no fear of using, right from their beginnings. It is enough for any young musician, however mediocre a *bâton-neur* he may be, to know an influential personality in order to 'be put into' an important position which he will retain indefinitely, unless people succeed in getting rid of him by paying him a handsome 'compensation'.

As for money, times have changed indeed. In the old days publishers could take advantage of the artists' excessive lack of interest in it. At last it was agreed to apply to Art as well as to Science the principle that each labourer is worthy of his hire. But 'the whirligig of time brings in his revenges', and many publishers today have cause to regret the pile of published scores which do not sell. The time has passed when Debussy himself, Ravel, Schmitt and many others had great difficulty in paying their annual subscription of twenty francs to the *Société Nationale* to give its annual orchestral concert. There is no longer any need for avant-garde societies. Cinema and radio have taken their place—and with what advantage for young composers! But also, with what danger to the aesthetic value of their works! Because we find that often the scores suggested to symphonic publishers for publication reveal in performance the inconsistency of hastily put-together 'incidental music' for films. Neither have young conductors to suffer debuts without payment, nor have they to 'ask of themselves more than they can achieve with ease'!

This commercialism and this lack of faith are the result of too many young people without any real vocation 'being put into' the musical profession. Hence the urgent need for that 'professional planning' we have advocated above.

People are too fond of repeating that in France we are lacking in outstanding personalities in all spheres. Most people carefully avoid noticing them, or if they cannot help it any longer, they meet them with hostility. But this does not prevent real leaders from at last imposing their will on others, be their names Gosset or Lyautey. 'What's the good?' has always been the excuse of the feeble or the incompetent. In French musical life there is, by the way, no lack of second-rate people, particularly since so many of them having risen to the very top. But when a real leader arises among the young, he will know how to find his place and how to keep it.

It will help him if he knows how to find, sometimes even outside his musical profession, examples which will teach him in his own art of music the science of how to behave and how to act, and of how to go about his duties. Let us quote again from Gosset's book rules which could be so appropriate for the conductor as well:

> The surgeon must be gifted with great natural skill. He will make few movements—never two when one is sufficient—and in each there will be a maximum of precision and efficiency. He must be calm, must watch everything and always be ready to adjust things with a movement which he must learn to do spontaneously, even before the mind has had time to think. He must possess a precise visual memory. He must remember former failures, but they must not make him a coward. He must develop the instinct of feeling things in advance. By watching others operate one can learn what to do as well as what not to do. He must be cautious and daring at the same time. He must have that indefinable quality—authority.

Authority!—virtue always associated with the real master, and lacking in so many *bâtonneurs*. With its innate moral force, authority confers:

> distrust for being flattered and for being criticized—more particularly for being flattered—and a great modesty combined with a very clear idea of his own value.

If he likes and knows how to read, a conductor will find in many other books analogies just as striking as the above . . . such as, for instance, the first phrase from the Hippocratic oath which ought to set all artists thinking, too: 'I swear to remain faithful to the laws of honour and integrity in the exercising of my profession'.

The real conductor, once he has found his right position, will endeavour to surround himself with assistants who have the right team spirit, giving them the appropriate authority and allowing them to share his responsibilities—without fear lest they abuse their power for egotistic purposes of their own—this often happens but never succeeds!

After more than thirty years of very fruitful team-work, my memory takes me back to a most moving communion of love of music, with inestimable collaborators . . . much more than to the few abortive cases of piracy.

VI. TRADUTTORE—TRADITORE

EVERY time we find ourselves in front of a classical score, we are struck by the difficulty of its performance and interpretation. The further we go back, the more difficult it becomes to recapture the composer's thoughts.

Since Beethoven, the indications of speed, of accents and of nuances have become more precise—sometimes even too much so. But further back? You hardly know what to take from the *forte* and *piano*, the only marks in the faithful Rameau republications which bear the names of Debussy, Fauré, and Dukas, and beyond which nothing else is *added*.

Crescendo and *diminuendo* are certain to have existed but were left to the performers' taste, just as before Bach and Couperin even the ornaments were not always marked by the composer, but left to the performer's imagination or his memory of verbal tradition. This explains the part played by taste—or the lack of it—in performing Bach or Mozart, whose works still set us problems which many mistakenly think are quite easy to solve.

Publishers evidently believed they were aiding the performer by publishing 'revisions' of past masterworks. Unfortunately this work has been entrusted too often to obscure, ignorant and vulgar hacks. Thus the interpreter's faith becomes trapped in worthless rubbish.

One of the world's most famous firms, Breitkopf & Haertel, which in two centuries has built up a monumental library, had specialized in republications of the classics. One would not dream of denying the importance of their work. Suffice it to mention that they undertook a complete Berlioz Edition, magnificently presented, and practically better than the French ones.

You may draw an even better comparison when remembering that the last 'French' edition of *La Damnation de Faust* has not only words *but even melodies* superimposed which a certain M. Gunsbourg inserted all through the famous score for his own scenic adaptation. As the French publisher published a pocket score according to this false edition, scandalously apocryphal words are met with, such as on page 77 where Faust intervenes to throw in two untimely *hosannas*. Although it is paradoxical, we have therefore now only a *German* edition to refer to, for the great *French* romantic composer's faithful text!

But while the Breitkopf & Haertel edition of Berlioz had been undertaken under the pious and alert direction of Felix Weingartner, that of the great classics had sometimes been done with the collaboration of revisers of doubtful credentials, often chosen from among simple violinists, *Konzertmeister* of some Philharmonie or another, in the defunct style of a method happy to clog the melodic line with marks for bowing and even for changing strings—which, in our opinion too, often likens Paganini's noble instrument to the Tyrolean piano-accordion. Consequently, this questionable style is even by its very text inevitably imposed upon our performers whenever they undertake to play a suite by Bach or a concerto by Mozart.

In order to re-establish the line of music in its original purity, long and patient work is necessary which mere faithfulness to the masters of Leipzig and Salzburg cannot replace. Only in this manner was I personally able to stick to scores which I had purged of the formidable additions of *bearbeitet von*. Guilmant's pupils used to say that in his class the master translated this as 'soiled by'.

On one of the rare occasions when I conducted the Orchestre de la Suisse Romande at Geneva, I happened to 'accompany'—as one puts it—a certain violinist from the other side of the Rhine, a man of great repute, in Mozart's A major concerto. On the day of the last rehearsal, the artist who had not hitherto deigned to introduce himself, entered solemn and stiff in his greatcoat, and discourteously looked me over through his monocle. After achieving contact in the *Allegro*, I began the charming string-passage of the *Andante*,

Andante du Concerto de Mozart

Andante of Mozart's A Major Concerto

when the soloist suddenly declared: 'A moment! You simply *must* play the first phrase like this, as I have to play it after you, and I play it like this.' And he scanned each group of two slurred notes, heavily stressing each first note:

'Oh', I replied in consternation. 'Is this how you play it? I'm afraid I am unable to do it that way, and as it is a *tutti*, I'll stick to my own style!' That night after the performance, I left the rostrum avoiding the traditional boxers' handshake and went off in the opposite direction to the soloist, a procedure I usually adopt in such cases. Next morning one could read these lines by the severest of Geneva critics which seemed to me like one of those rare cases of justice: 'It was of major interest to hear a Latin showing a Teuton how to interpret Mozart'.

This story confirms the lack of understanding of uncultured revisers who do not hesitate to break the pure *cantando* of a simple melody by means dictated by the technique of the

D

instrument. The numerous types of bowing and stressing in the first Kreutzer study were solely contrived for the ease of the violinist's right arm. Adapted indiscriminately to performance, they often destroy the composer's idea.

The question of how to interpret the classics can be forever the subject of argument. Also, in particular, 'specialized' interpreters must be met with caution. The masters of the past have no means of defending their ideas against abuses, no matter what charlatan sets up his fantastic interpretation as a tradition. A short time before the end of the period between the two world wars, when cynicism had free play, nothing less than the menacing ultimatum from redoubtable Mozartians was required to prevent an official ceremony at Versailles, at which a questionable violinist was to play for the first time an apocryphal Mozart concerto on a spurious 'Mozart violin'. If archaeologists must sometimes be mistrusted, one must always doubt those specialized interpreters, cynical revisers and commentators of works of the past who under the pretence of being antiquaries are not even ordinary second-hand dealers, but just junk-merchants.

What should one say about Beethoven 'visionaries' who superimpose on the nine symphonies their nuances, their slowing-down of the melodic themes in contrast to the 'go' of the rhythmical themes? Up till now the example of the *Herren Kapellmeister* was followed also in France, without ever reflecting that Beethoven always marked his speed with precision—and often with a metronome. He would not have failed to mark those fluctuations, of pace as well, if he had wanted them. Other traditions, those of Habeneck for example, are just as indefensible. Let us always remember Berlioz' words: 'The singer has often been accused of being the most dangerous intermediary between composer and public; in my opinion, the greatest danger is the conductor'.

What about this other Beethovenian 'tradition' which consists in doubling the woodwind under the pretext of re-estab-

lishing the balance of orchestration in the symphonies, taking
into consideration our modern number of strings, claimed as
indispensable for the dimensions of our concert halls? Did
anyone ever have the idea of doubling or trebling the number
of four strings if a quartet performance of works by Mozart or
Franck or Debussy is given in the Salle Gaveau, the Opéra, or
even in the Garage Pleyel?

After the Armistice of 1918, I undertook with some willing
musicians to play the works of the past with reduced orchestra.
In the dear old Salle Pleyel—the true one—I reproduced the
exact Dresden orchestra model of Hasse who once performed
Haydn's symphonies there. Nothing could be more natural
than this reconstruction. Anyone can find in J. J. Rousseau's
musical encyclopaedia or in Riemann's dictionary the precise
indication of the number of strings.

*Distribution de l'Orchestre de l'Opera de Dresde,
Dirigé par le S: Hasse.*

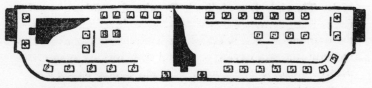

Renvois des Chiffres.

1. Clavecin du Maître de Chapelle
2. Clavecin d'accompagnement
3. Violoncelles.
4. Contre - basses.
5. Premiers Violons
6. Second Violons, ayant le dos
   tourné vers le Théâtre.

7. Hautbois, de même.
8. Flutes, de même.
a. Tailles, de même.
b. Bassons.
c. Cors de Chasse.
d. Une Tribune de Chaque côté pour les
   Tymballes et Trompettes.

Distribution of the Opera Orchestra in Dresden.
Conducted by Signor Hasse.

1 Conductor's Cembalo
2 Accompanist's Cembalo
3 'Celli
4 Double-basses
5 First Violins
6 Second Violins, with their backs to the audience.

7 Oboes, ditto
8 Flutes, ditto
a Violas, ditto
b Bassoons
c Horns (without valves)
d A gallery on each side for Tympani and Trumpets.

A little later I experimented with the same set-up in the Théâtre des Champs-Elysées, comparing the sound with that of a modern-sized orchestra, in a Mozart symphony. The experiment was so conclusive that henceforth I adopted this reform which simple reasoning ought to have recommended a long time ago. But this is the way of the world. Even among the most famous conductors, very few seem ever to have considered balance in this manner: in Haydn's and Mozart's as well as in Beethoven's early symphonies the upper part is played by the violins, the lower part is generally doubled—'celli and double-basses—and sometimes even trebled by the violas. The eight first violins in Dresden thus did not run the risk of being drowned by the two basses, three 'celli, and even the four violas. But what of the sixteen first violins of the modern orchestra having to defend their melody against the massive offensive of eighteen 'celli and double-basses, sometimes reinforced by ten or twelve violas?

Following the same idea, the plan of Hasse's model orchestra indicates the precise position of the harpsichord (cembalo) which the conductor, while conducting, often used for recitatives and for completing or strengthening the harmony by playing the *continuo*. But the Breitkopf edition gives for all Bach works not one but two distinct cembalo parts, the execution of which only makes the polyphony heavy.

The comparison of republications with the original text is often impossible. Therefore it is a wise conductor's duty to know how to distinguish between those of the printed instructions which he can allow himself to follow and those which ought to be disregarded. Correct reasoning alone should be the judge of the inevitable standardization of nuances and accents. It is not enough to give the orchestra its correct strength for Bach, Haydn, and Mozart. One must also grade the accents, not only in the differences between the *sforzando* in a *forte* and in a *piano*, but by weakening these accents in depth, through a kind of 'vertical diminuendo', resulting sometimes in the suppression of certain accents in the basses, for the benefit of the upper instruments and especially of the melodic line.

These remarks are not confined to classical works but are equally valid for the interpretation of all music. Our 'vertical diminuendo' and the limitation of strings apply also to the *Siegfried Idyll* and the *Pavane pour une Infante Défunte*, to *Masques et Bergamasques* and the Scherzo from *A Midsummer Night's Dream*.

Concerning what we have said about the habitual uniformity of dynamics, we may make another observation of the same order. In strongly contrapuntal polyphonic works and in those with certain dissonant harmonic progressions, composers rarely think of providing a different gradation for each individual part of the counterpoint or of the dissonant harmonies. In performance, the result will be confusion, making it difficult for the listener to understand, as the difference of timbre is insufficient to avoid this drawback. Then it will be the conductor's task to underline *slightly* those themes or dissonant parts which he thinks ought to be prominent in a more transparent texture. This method is in principle identical with the 'vertical diminuendo' advocated above.

Indications of speed, accents, and dynamics have become ever more precise and ever more numerous—sometimes even to excess—and ever grows the danger of confusing letter and spirit. For often composers themselves have been guilty of

confusing the real meaning of these signs, this musicians'
Esperanto. And very many revisers of the works of the past
have only confirmed them in their error.

In order to recapture the spirit of the composers throughout
their works, the conductor more than any other interpreter
must know how properly to distinguish between what must
be followed to the letter and what can be disregarded. He must
also distrust oral traditions which may haunt his memory and
must deal with great caution also with his own personal
temptation to reform.

My unhappy predecessor at the Opéra-Comique, a *graffiti-
addict*, used to declare gravely, rolling his Toulouse 'r', that
he had just 'de-greased' *Carmen*, or 're-greased' *Orfeo*. It so
happened that in the course of these operations his 'logic' induced him to change the dramatically so characteristic few
little 2-4 bars when Don José ties Carmen's hands while
Zuniga goes away. (No. 9 of the score.) Poor fellow, he was
unable to feel the impact of progressive emptiness around the
two lovers-to-be, or the quiet after the tumult, depicted by
Bizet's genius simply by stating the motif in binary instead of
in ternary rhythm. So he simply changed them back into the
ternary rhythm in which they generally appear and in which,
so he fondly believed, they ought to appear in this passage,
too!

It might seem incredible that anyone should thus change the
music under the pretext of correcting it. This impertinence is
mostly characteristic of the young: jealous of the experience
of older people, beginners will try hard to find fault with
them. And this sometimes induces them to blunder badly.
One of the worst cases is worth telling here, as a warning.

During a rehearsal of Chabrier's *Suite Pastorale* with the
Orchestre Nationale I had arrived at the third piece, the
moving *Sous-Bois*. Just before the double-bar before the
resumption of the theme, in the gentle ascending passage on
the pedal-point of the dominant, on the second beat of the

sixty-first bar of the piece, I suddenly heard a terribly wrong
note in the melody—and was surprised at seeing the orchestra
smile, waiting for what I would say. Throwing a quick glance
at the score I saw that an enormous 'sharp' had been inserted
with red pencil in front of the C of the flute and the first
violins and, in the margin, a *graffito* saying that there had been
a mistake here as the piano edition showed a sharp, now and
herewith transferred into the full score.

Although I had heard the interpretation of this piece more
than forty years ago by one of Chabrier's closest associates,
and although I had myself conducted it innumerable times,
and, above all, although the C sharp was intolerable to the ear,
I was worried by the explanation given at the margin, coming
as it did from a young conductor known to be anything but
an ignoramus, winner of an authentic Grand Prix de Rome,
who died a short while afterwards.

So I got from Enoch's, the publishers, the collection for
piano called *Dix pièces pittoresques*, extracts from which form
the *Suite Pastorale* for orchestra, and there and then discovered
the 'sharp' engraved distinctly before the C. However, remembering the precise picture of Litolff's original edition

which was presented in an altogether different manner—but which I did not possess any more—I submitted the whole case to my amazing assistant Emile Passani who sat down at the piano, played the whole piece from memory, with C *natural*, and also brought me his copy of an earlier edition which showed the jump of a minor tenth, without the spurious alteration.

Would not this comparison between two texts demonstrate an equal incompetence on the part of conductor, publisher and reviser alike? Thinking of the official qualifications of the conductor, one remains nonplussed . . . still another proof of the differences in the susceptibility of musicians' ears and the lack of harmonic understanding of some of them.

In a charming film *Jean de la Lune*, one of the characters, the Bohemian Cloco, deafens the others with his songs and explains that though his singing is wrong, his hearing is right! There seem to be, alas, among musicians some poor wretches whose playing *and* hearing are wrong! Moreover, this inclination for consulting piano scores might well conceal the shortcomings of those who are incapable of *hearing* an orchestral score merely by reading it. The method of working with a piano score is as pernicious for conductors as beating time in front of a mirror for imaginary players.

Another beginner exposed his ignorance in Liszt's *Mephisto-Waltz* by suppressing the twenty-fifth bar of the *poco moderato* which, according to his *graffito*, was superfluous as it did not exist in the piano edition. He failed to understand that the very orchestration with its successive entries indicated that at this particular passage the composer, when orchestrating this work primarily meant for piano, had preferred to postpone by one bar the modulation to A flat and the statement of the second theme, at letter 'D'.

The library of Radio Paris thoughtlessly entrusts its scores to all sorts of conductors and shows too much tolerance towards their fancy scribblings. Thus I discovered in my own works some 'corrections' made by people who nobly intended to suppress mistakes, and instead had added some.

There is no need to invent mistakes! One can find enough real ones—in *Faust*, for example. I discovered glaring mistakes in *Pelléas* during my first appointment at the Opéra-Comique, more than twenty years after the first performance. Would this imply a retrospective blame on the auditory qualities of Messager or Debussy? Not at all! At the same time and place I unearthed in the first scene of my *Pénélope* a terribly wrong note in a simple chord of the seventh, ten years after the first performance. Revising the orchestration of the latter score in view of its revival at the Opéra in 1949, I found almost two hundred uncorrected mistakes in the orchestra parts. The most important mistake in *Pelléas* is on page 210 of the orchestral score, on the last beat of the last bar. The last crotchet of the first horn in F must be an E natural and the last small note of the glockenspiel must be an A natural.

In *Pénélope* the most serious mistake is not in the score but in one of the horn parts. In the second bar of page 16, piano score, corresponding with the fourth bar, page 30, of the full score, the dotted minim C belonging to the two chords on the first and second beat is played by the third horn in F. The horn part shows an A instead of a G. And in both these scores one will find still other mistakes in reference to which it will be said one day that I myself had not 'heard' them previously.

One must also distrust some of our very best orchestral musicians who are in the habit of correcting mistakes while playing, either by instinct or from memory, but who omit entering these corrections into their parts.

The most efficient way of finding errors and mistakes is to make the orchestra play not only slowly, but also *piano*. For in *forte*, and especially as heard from the conductor's place, some inaccuracies may elude even the most subtle ear. It has always surprised me that this method is not employed more frequently. It may be possible, besides, that this method con-

stitutes a means of preserving delicate eardrums from premature deafness.

On the other hand, one often forgets mistakes which one
has heard in performance; or rather, a later search for them
will be in vain. When one cannot write them down while
conducting, one might with the left hand slip little bookmarks
between the pages so that doubtful passages may be found
later.

To sum up: the respect for the text must be 'intelligent'. It
is solely a matter for a conductor's culture and wisdom to
look at 'the letter' with circumspect deference. But alas! it
would be the exact reverse of what one ought to do, were we
always rigidly to observe all the spurious accents of the *bear-
beitung* or those superfluous ones of certain composers such as
Schumann or Chabrier, for example. It is thus that splitting
up of the musical line will persist, caused by the incoherence
of the slurs and the confusion between *détaché* and *staccato* in
the strings. By way of contrast, marks of composers who
knew how to show their intentions with perfect clarity are
observed either not at all or insufficiently.

We can never mistrust ourselves enough on this latter
point! Just fancy this: speaking of *Carmen*, Toscanini made
some remark which I thought very wise—which made him
add, smilingly: 'But it's in your book!' Then he went on to
quote the *erroneous* tradition of making the horns blare out
the tragic reappearance of the Carmen theme, twenty-eight
bars before the end of the third act. He insisted it was usually
the fault of the woodwind, the oboes in particular, in neglecting to play *fortissimo*, adding that in any case oboes in unison
were simply bound to be 'recalcitrant'. And then I discovered
that I myself had forgotten to mention this wrong tradition
and that I had even allowed myself for a long time to let the
horns compensate for the nonchalance of the oboes by letting
them play more brassily!

It is the musicians' noble task to redress the bad and false traditions in the repertoire works. I have tried to indicate the majority of those which abound in *Faust*, in *Carmen*, and already in *Pelléas*.

Interpretations of *Pelléas* already depart more and more from the 'spirit' of Debussy, and the posters of the Opéra-Comique have even added a new character, hitherto unknown, 'the little shepherd', sung by a high baritone whose voice resembles that of Pelléas. But the passage that was meant was merely the simple phrase answering from off-stage the questioning of little Yniold, and the roughness of tone must contrast with the fragility of the child's voice, underlining one of the drama's symbols. Therefore, from the first performance on, the passage was sung by the singer of the Doctor of the fifth act; whereas the innovators seem to have confused the invisible character with the charming 'little shepherd' of *Children's Corner*.

In the same manner, stage-directions and scenery had to be 'modernized' when Albert Carré was no longer director. When I asked him at that time what he thought of the scenery, he answered: 'Yes, yes, we know all that: a forest is replaced by a kitchen-garden . . . but we must allow the new brooms the time to gather experience.'

We shall often see kitchen-gardens replacing forests during this period of penance which art is undergoing all over the world. We could quote the urgent need for sanity in thousands of cases if we had the time. In order to seize just one opportunity let it be sufficient to analyse only the beginning of *Lakmé*. How often did we have to listen to Delibes' masterwork being massacred in the following manner.

From the first bar of the prelude on, we knew what to think of the great vigour of the musicians and of their servant, the conductor; it was one of those evenings when the supposed lion-tamer descended into the den, very careful not to offend its occupants by orders.

With the first beat of the first bar we learned that a double-dotted quaver need not end, as we had hitherto believed, in a demisemiquaver, but in a value vaguely brief and unclassifiable. The second beat indicated that if two demisemiquavers in anacrucis produce the vague idea of a semiquaver-triplet, it is quite sufficient. A dotted crotchet of the trombone need not be sustained longer than for scarcely one beat, in order to have time for a breath. The third beat saw its last quaver shortened, undoubtedly in opposition to all the short values which had been lengthened!

All this was revealed to us in the course of this one first bar. Following less 'closely', we noticed nevertheless that the dry *fortissimo* chords on the third beat of each fourth bar were feeble and soft. So we arrived at the *Andante*. The violins, exhausted by their efforts, did not adopt the *decrescendo* for passing from *forte* to *pianissimo*, but let the *mezzoforte* which is all they had achieved drift vaguely into a *mezzopiano*. It was agreed that we would not put ourselves out for the sake of the pauses and halts, but that on the contrary, rests would be shortened in order to gain time. The strings crushed the approaching duet theme—which was also taken up 'in force' by the woodwind. Thus, the end was arrived at, without our being able to catch the meaning of that magnificent chromatic rise of the Dourga theme, its robust *crescendo* to the *fortissimo*, then the mysterious *piano-pizzicati* at half-speed . . . a long silence . . . and at last, without any haste, up went the curtain.

But there had not been any singing yet! There were going to be choirs—they were reciting their prayers to Brahma, whose temple and image were at the back—and facing the conductor, turning their back on the god, they performed their rites. And then the singers: the attendant Malika sang sharp in her duet with Lakmé, who sang flat; the 'interlude of the fifes' would be muddled, the 'Nilakantha stanzas' would die away, and the 'bell-song' would be hustled. There was the ballet with its Hindu dancers wearing their wrist-watches, the rotund star-dancer, also Hindu, dancing her number on her points, her bosom adorned by the classical diamond brooch which she refuses to discard, no matter what her rôle. Later, there would be Gerald, who would sustain so interminably the 'wee . . hee . . hee . . hings' of his love that a shudder would run through the spectators asking themselves whether a dislocated jaw would perhaps condemn the frisky British officer to remain hee-haw-ing for the rest of his life.

For *Le Roi d'Ys*, too, it is a struggle right from the start. There was a time when the most provincial of Paris managers had put this warning on the poster of the Opéra-Comique, before the name of the solo 'cellist: 'No admittance during the famous overture'!. . . too famous indeed, and too popular at all the seaside bandstands!

At the beginning of the *Allegro*, the string melody is interrupted by untimely rests

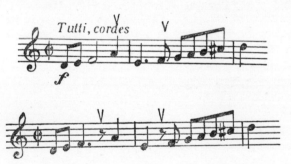

owing to the fact that the players will not sustain the long tones on the down-bow. They will interrupt their sound by rests, instead of only by the up-bow of the short tones.

The conductor has to watch that the players don't draw the bow too far at the syncopated passages in order to be able to begin the following note without interrupting the *legato*.

At Margaret's phrase 'Lorsque je t'ai vu soudain reparaître vivant . . .' the strings usually play with all their force, whereas the score says that there is to be a *pianissimo* for twelve bars, later to swell only to *mezzoforte* before, even later still, a *forte* is reached. Scraping away at full force, too, the 'cellist will transform the *Andantino non troppo* of his too-famous solo into a *Largo*. Nose on his strings, he will obstinately glue his eyes on the bridge, thus avoiding being importuned by the conductor's efforts at preventing him from dragging.

In the *Barber of Seville* we have to take our stand against the traditional 'near enough' from the very first note on. As with the majority of anacruces, this first note is usually played with lack of care. A demisemiquaver instead of a simple semiquaver will be the result. However, there must never be any haphazard way of making music, only the responsible task of playing correctly and in correct rhythm.

But all this gives only the impression of trailers shown in the cinema in the interval, advertising next week's film. We should like one day to see the whole film. And there are *Le Roi d'Ys, Mireille, Werther, Manon,* and so many other 'minor' masterworks of the repertoire, the beauty of which it is sometimes not possible even to suspect any longer.

If one departs too far from the text it is a proof that one does not understand what the composer meant. How many conductors remind us of the young man who had stuffed himself full of themes and translations in a foreign language which he neither spoke nor understood and who in despair explained: 'I was taught all that was necessary to pass examinations but that's no help!'

It is necessary to go beyond rules in order to understand. Certain *bâtonneurs* have remained stationary at some musical period and everything that happened later passes them by. The majority cling to Romanticism and to Bizet, Franck, and Lalo. One of these Metronomi spoke to his orchestra about a Debussy score and said with a disdainful smile: 'Let's tackle that *thing* there!'—One must not lose sight of the fact that people like this have usually tried their hand at composing in vain. The same man used to conduct the finale of the second act of *Carmen* right through at the metronome speed of 80 to the dotted crochet, evidently marked by Bizet, but undoubtedly wrong, as one can and *must* realize at the beginning of the 6-8 at the end of the *Flower Song*. Otherwise, José will take his beautiful girl far away, far away into the mountains on a shortwinded old hack. Metronomus simply does not understand any more of Bizet than of Debussy, Berlioz, Wagner or Mozart.

Some of the preceding lines might seem contradictory in that we have been proclaiming all the time the need for respect of the text and its 'interpretation'. But haven't we also said quite clearly that it must be an 'intelligent' respect? There is an opposite to everything that exists. Our art is full of contradictions, owing to the very fact that according to the nature of the works different types of interpretation are possible; this is how advice for interpreters may sometimes seem contradictory. Those who are able to, will understand. Those who want to, will learn. And those who are pig-headed don't matter.

Just as the conductor-composer will understand better than others the composers' intentions, so the composer-conductor will write down his intentions better than others. One has only to remember the scores of Mendelssohn, Weber, Wagner, Berlioz and Liszt, and their writings about their composing or their activity as conductors. Liszt especially gives in his scores the impression of the real and conscientious conductor-composer. It even seems that he has put the guiding letters of his scores in scientific places! His remarks and reflections at the beginning of his works and at the bottom of the pages, his innovation of indicating long *accelerandi* and *ritardandi* by the first few letters of these words, followed by dots until the end of the acceleration or the retarding, are meant to be precautions against the all-too-frequent shortcomings of those he himself dubbed *bâtonneurs*.

But overdoing things being harmful, we have also to admit

that his *non crescendo* or *non diminuendo* which other composers later applied in their turn, rarely brings about the expected reaction on the part of the players. As a matter of fact, as a natural result of their custom of reading 'ahead', they will pass over the first of these two words to the second. It is familiar to them and will even induce them to produce the very increase or decrease of tone-volume they were intended to avoid.

The fine conductor can be judged from his correct 'realization' of the dynamic marks. We know the old joke of the conductor who, having asked his musicians to play *forte*, recommences again and again, all the time renewing his exhortation until the man at the big drum has smashed his instrument—only then does the conductor declare that he had certainly asked for *forte* but not for *fortissimo*!

To a great extent it is the influence of the mechanical age which in certain pieces brings about dynamism in music, and under a distant influence of impressionism, avant-garde musicians before the first world-war have exalted motor-car, locomotive, and factory in their symphonic works. The natural consequence was to experiment with new means of expression which only produce noise. This explains the imitations of the back-firing of a motor-cycle, and the monstrous hornet-noise of the speed-boat. Hence also some new electronic musical instruments which are noisily publicised and succeed in sometimes introducing into scores a lamentable *glissando*.

But we need not waste any more time with these discoveries than with the lucubrations of 'imitation-composers' lacking technique and inspiration. It would be all too easy for these delinquents to call our attitude lack of understanding of the kind shown to all innovators. Have not Meyerbeer after *Les Huguenots*, and Gounod after *Faust* been called 'knights of the wrong note', like Berlioz, Wagner, and Debussy?

We are thinking rather of certain works by real musicians, masters whom we love and admire, so excited by polyphonic power to the degree that they have overstepped the capacity for auditory perception on the part of their public. For we do not mean, in this case, scores which burst the frame in which they are presented, stifled by the small dimensions of a concert hall. We are referring rather to unrestrained power which purely produces noise whatever the acoustic conditions, even in an open-air concert. It is of obstinate persistence in *fortissimo*, as horrifying as the motor-horns which tear at our ear-drums in the street and make us afraid of sudden deafness.

The executants are even worse off. Generally speaking, the orchestral musician, part of a whole, is bound to misunderstand sometimes the ensemble of what he is playing. But in the end he will perceive the emerging line and anyway be aware of the usefulness of his participation. This feeling of usefulness will vanish in the case of the supertension we have mentioned. As deafened as the bell-ringer in his steeple, wearied by his own inability to discern the slightest detail, it will seem useless to him to 'take the plunge'. This may go so far that some of the players will be unable to resist the temptation of playing 'just anything' in order to watch whether 'it will be heard'. In fact, we have to confess 'it won't be'! The rôle of the conductor is just as depressing and this is the very occasion on which he has to recourse to rehearsing *pianissimo* in order to be able to hear for himself and to separate the tares from the wheat. If this were applied more often, a lesser number of gross mistakes would remain in the scores.

There are really cases when we might extend to music the use of those 'ear-plugs' for protecting air-travellers from the noise of the engines.

Composers do not give a thought to the fact that a musical performance lacks the advantage of 'taking a second look' which is possible in the other arts. In order to help your understanding, you may walk around a statue, you can examine

E

some detail of a painting, and you can read twice the obscure passages of a book. But music, once it has been played, is over, because only the professionals are able to read twice through a score in order to pierce the obscurity of the dark places or to dwell on some detail, like the archaeologist on that of a mediaeval porch. It was said that Chabrier, asked why he always wrote with pencil, replied: 'In order to be able to change it!' The correct procedure is to clarify by weeding out. By excessive harmonic richness and by superabundance of queer ideas, the composer of *Le Roi malgré lui* and of *Gwendoline* confused his public.

These are the subtleties which escape interpreters most frequently: the differentiation between *mezzoforte* and *piano*, between *piano* and *pianissimo*, the correct change from one of these dynamic marks to the other, from loud to soft as well as vice versa. Especially the frequent changes from *pianissimo* to *piano* are rarely observed in the way that the listener becomes aware of them. In that temperate zone of *piano* and *mezzopiano* we meet with the greatest difficulty of dynamic differentiation —it becomes, one might say, locked in the mind of the interpreter.

In his book *Temps et Contretemps* Gustave Doret quotes these lines by Saint-Saëns:

> Since you are training conductors, try to make them lose that habit, now becoming general, of making every *piano* a *pianissimo*. When there is *piano*, the strings play with one hair of the bow; there is no life, no colour. Tell them also there are several sorts of Allegro: Allegro moderato, Allegro non troppo, poco Allegro, Allegro quasi Allegretto, Allegro animato, Allegro molto, Allegro presto. For many conductors—and not the worst ones, either—only the last-mentioned counts: Allegro presto. Under the pretext of giving warmth, they start running. To begin with, speed is not necessarily warmth. Secondly, music has some other things to express, besides warmth. But speed is supposed to express everything, from placid calm to dishevelled passion. To put warmth of this kind into everything is absurd.

To this reprimand of the master, concerning 'untimely warmth' which is a sort of hysteria with musicians, we may add that it is often caused by incessant string-vibrato. This means of expression would otherwise be efficient if employed with more moderation, especially by 'celli and double-bass players who abuse it immoderately.

For example, transition from *piano* to *pianissimo* may be most perfectly achieved by simply cutting out the vibrato— and vice versa. This absolute suppression of vibrato is indispensable in order to give to a *pianissimo* all its grandeur, its impression of 'perfect calm', as Saint-Saëns says. Here are two striking examples: the string-unison at the beginnings of the *Andante* of the *Symphony with Organ*, and the first bars of the overture of *Le Roi d'Ys*.

In one case only do string players change their extravagance of vibrato into a puritan non-vibrato: when they interpret Bach or Beethoven. They just have this slightly oversimplified way of expressing their respect for the classics—for these two, at least. They even go as far as hardening the tone a little, as if to withdraw from it all the charm it might have. They are, then, possessed with the same urge of humility which makes a courtesan take off her make-up before entering a church.

It seems that Lucien Capet forced his pupils to play Beethoven's *Romance in F* from beginning to end without vibrato which was right only from the point of view of technique. Toscanini, on the other hand, irritated by this method, replied that before becoming classics, Bach and Beethoven had been moderns themselves.

A judicious employment of vibrato may allow quite unsuspected subtlety of expression, but all the string players would have to agree to carry out the conductor's directions and this is infinitely rare. Under the influence of jazz, even the wind instruments, too, have adopted the use of vibrato, seduced by unrestrained saxophone sentimentality.

The following error may often be observed: when there is a *crescendo* between *pianissimo* and *piano*, and when this *crescendo* has been taken to a point where the tone-volume has exceeded the *piano*, the mistake will be compensated by the conductor in this manner: having allowed the orchestra to arrive at what might be *mezzoforte*, he will then conduct a *subito piano*, thus interrupting the line of expression by a brusque regression—and this, although the *piano* marked in the score was meant purely and simply as the result, ending point, and issue of the *crescendo* preceding it. Thus, the wings of a moving expansion are clipped by a lack of understanding as to how to keep it completely within the bounds dictated by the composer. A typical example exists in the last bars of the *Andante* of Beethoven's 'Pastoral' Symphony in the course of which the conductor must prevent himself from following the habitual reflex of the *subito piano*, dictated by a false tradition.

At this bar the tradition is to extinguish sonority. This is wrong. It should have been done five bars earlier.

If it were necessary to confirm this example by its replica, its sister-example, one could find it in the third movement of Brahms' Second Symphony:

2nd Symphony by Brahms.

Allegretto grazioso.

But generally, we shall only give one example typical of each 'case' and will leave it to the reader's curiosity and initiative to find out where else it applies as well.

If it is difficult for beginners to execute dymanics properly, they are no less difficult for the composer himself to mark. Even many of the masters did not succeed. This takes us to the point where the conductor, in order to find out what they really did mean, has even to apply the opposite of what is marked. Debussy and Brahms, for example, put dots over those string-notes which they wanted to be *détaché*. They well knew, of course, that this dot means originally *sautillé* or *staccato*, but that there is no sign in music which indicates *détaché*. In order to obviate errors of indication or interpretation in this respect, I adopted a long time ago *strings détaché*. With regard to the proper *sautillé*, instrumentalists often overdo it, and thus hack the melody to pieces by incorrect phrasing. They also commit the error of anticipating the effect of the dot placed over the note. In the two following examples which are typical, a cross indicates the place where, as a result of this mistake, a rest is inserted between a long note, which ought to be sustained, and the staccato note which ought to follow it without interruption.

Scherzo from *Midsummer Night's Dream* by Mendelssohn.

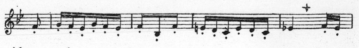

Scherzo du "Songe d'une Nuit d'Eté" de Mendelssohn

(the same later, in E flat, and later in G.)

Forlane du "Tombeau de Couperin" de Ravel

The wind instruments' phrasing is often indicated in a completely erroneous and arbitrary manner. In the Funeral March of the 'Eroica' at the oboe entry in the ninth bar, the theme is hacked to pieces and loses its character unless the conductor induces the player to rectify the text by starting the phrase at its beginning instead of where it is marked.

Funeral March from Beethoven's 'Eroica'.
(Oboe Entry)

The uniformity of dynamics for the whole orchestra is a danger to the performance unless the conductor measures the dynamics according to the character of the instruments and according to the character of what they have to play—unless, expressing it briefly, he 'adapts' them according to the precedence of melody and essential harmony. But this requires some time and some cautious pondering, and our musicians of today are so much in a hurry that some composers have adopted the deplorable habit of marking dynamics with one bold stroke, with one single line of large characters right across the centre of the page. 'Time is money.' How far have we departed from the days when Flaubert wrote to the *young* Guy de Maupassant: 'For an artist, there exists only one principle: to sacrifice everything to his art. Life itself must be considered by him as nothing more than a means to an end!'

One must have time for reflecting. And one must have a flair for reflecting in order gradually to discover those errors of interpretation which have ultimately set themselves up as traditions. In this way, you will never get tired of performing the same familiar scores again and again, and of re-examining them every time. This is how you will find out the error, so current at the present time, of making all the dynamic changes always uniform in the Gavotte from Bach's Suite in D; the basses usually begin their *forte* on the second half of the first bar (of the second reprise) with the whole orchestra, whereas if they start playing *forte* on the B (at the beginning of the bar as marked in the example) they then show up the thematic imitation by underlining it in advance, as it were.

Gavotte from the Suite in D by Bach
Gavotte de la Suite en Ré de Bach

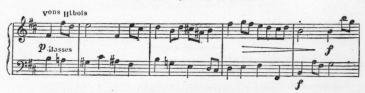

Here it was a question of well-reasoned disregard of the printed mark. But we also give here a clear case where disregard of the text is wrong, and is commonly found—in the finale of Lalo's *Symphonie Espagnole*. Throughout the whole movement, at each return of the theme, the composer clearly indicated that after an easy *ritenuto* the soloist must resume *a tempo* on the second quaver of the second beat, with what are the first two notes of the theme. Which, of course, does not prevent any violinist from lingering on these two notes as if they still belonged to the *ritenuto*, against all logic, just following their taste, or rather, their bad taste!

Symphonie espagnole de Lalo
(Final)

But generally speaking, Lalo's music is not always well served by too scrupulous observation of the dynamics. The marks are often exaggerated, particularly in *Le Roi d'Ys*, where the balance between voice and orchestra is always against the voice. The accentuations are too numerous as in Chabrier. And although he played a stringed instrument himself Lalo, like Debussy, Brahms, and so many others, puts dots on top of the notes to indicate a simple *détaché à la corde*.

Debussy, who deeply admired Lalo, had a predilection for *Namouna*, the fairy-tale atmosphere of which has remained intact and will always conquer us anew, despite its age. The first orchestral suite is a selection taken from the ballet. But like so many other masterworks in the repertoire, it has become so popular that nearly all performances bristle with spurious traditions. To purge the work it would have to be rehearsed conscientiously, taken to pieces like an unknown work, and like a difficult one, at that—because of its technical difficulties. Certain details of the *Prélude*, the *Thème varié*, and the *Parades de Foire* even demand patient and repeated rehearsing at reduced speed, with the strings. Gradually the *ritenuti* and *rubati* of the charming flute solo have been multiplied, and the hunting horns which Debussy loved so much are seldom as predominant as the composer wanted them. As with so many other works, including Beethoven's symphonies, performances of *Namouna* suffer from a deplorable slovenliness. In our days no one deigns to *read* these scores any more, they are played just in the manner in which they have always been heard. Often they are not even being rehearsed, owing to the lack of time. More and more do orchestras and conductors ignore the fact that despite many performances a score remains always like the eternally unfinished tapestry of Penelope.

It is wrong, of course, to have referred previously to the boredom you *might* feel at playing again the most familiar scores. When they are perfect masterworks they can stand the test of time and you never become satiated with them.

As a humble second violinist of fifteen years of age, in the Concerts de l'Opéra, I felt the colossal revelation of *Namouna*, *La Damnation de Faust*, and especially of the third *Leonora* overture. After fifty years I still cannot conduct or hear the latter work without feeling my heart rent as on the first day, and without tears coming into my eyes with the rising of hope which follows the trumpet signals. When we talked about it, one day, Toscanini told me the real 'revelation' he had had one night when *listening* at the Scala to a *Fidelio* performance. Thinking of the famous violin passage before it occurred, he told himself suddenly: 'This must be a D!' And when the C was played, it almost choked him. A little later he found among trustworthy documents the confirmation of his intuition. Thinking about this, I read again Weingartner's booklet, *The Art of Conducting*, in which he alludes to—and tries to disprove —Hans von Bülow's idea which confirms Toscanini's intuition. Ever since I have voted for D: it would belong in a natural manner to the suspended dominant. The suspended dominant, maintained till the *tutti*, would be more logical than if heavily interrupted by the anticipation of the resolution on this contentious first quaver. I believe that the partisans of this modification would be unable to bear any longer the C, consecrated by text and usage. But one could also perfectly understand if others stick to a tradition confirmed by the text.

This is really only an honest controversy among loyal servants of music. Alas, this does not often occur. Had not some cunning pianist, about to play the Schumann concerto with me, suggested using *her* orchestral score? I replied I would use the one by *Schumann* and that I deemed it quite sufficient for both of us. This elicited an angry reply: 'One cannot always give standardized performances!' 'The standardization of the Schumann concerto', I replied, 'is no mean feat, and is not easy!' The incessant rubato of the senora, *her* dynamics and *her* contortions had to be seen and heard to be believed.

Every time we let ourselves go with unmarked speed-fluctuations, we give the proof that we have failed to meet the composer's intentions, and that we are using a trick to save ourselves. The noisy woman had forgotten—if indeed she had ever read it—this remark by Schumann himself: 'The playing of certain pianists reminds me of the staggering of someone who is drunk'.

In contrast to the escapades of the Commedianti of the keyboard and of the bow, there is always agreement between loyal interpreters. An Yves Nat, a Robert Casadesus, or a Gieseking, playing with me the Schumann or any concerto by Beethoven, Liszt, or Mozart, has never been afraid of standardizing himself in the same manner as I, namely, adopting the composer's speeds.

Here it is a question of intelligence in the subtle relation of personality and conscientious but not blind respect for the text. It is often ignorance which lies at the basis of conflicts between interpreters.

Presiding over a jury for the selection of bandmasters for the Air Force, I was surrounded by the most eminent specialists. One of the tests consisted in orchestrating a simple minuet written by one of the members of the jury. Correcting the manuscripts, I noticed to my great surprise that the majority of the competitors had abused percussion in a manner irreconcilable with the character of the piece. Then my colleagues of the Army revealed that the developments due to Gabriel Parès and Pierre Dupont—to name only the greatest celebrities— had not yet been universally adopted and that some of the competitors had stuck to the old type of orchestration where percussion *had* to be applied all the time to maintain the rhythm. And I found also that the only military band orchestration of the *Figaro* overture in existence offered us fatheads of the symphony orchestra this neo-Mozartian idea:

Overture to 'The Marriage of Figaro'
Ouverture des Noces de Figaro

I am not mentioning this with any ironic intent, because symphonists have done worse than that: I remember having heard in a film a famous Haydn minuet in which a saxophone added to our delight—of course, purely in order to provide royalties for the arranger!

There are in existence many excellent brass band arrangements of symphonic masterworks which have been done with infinite and scrupulous care. We have to add, by the way, that most of the observations contained in this book apply to brass bands as well as to the symphony orchestra.

VII. PSYCHOLOGY

NIKISCH, so it is said, was of the opinion that the control of a conductor over his musicians was partially of a psychological nature and depended on the knowledge of their idiosyncrasies according to the instrument they play. The celebrated *Kapellmeister* said that clarinettists are inclined to be sentimental: they must be talked to with infinite gentleness. Musicians who play the viola or any of the big brass instruments get through their very playing a strong atmosphere of calmness and a constant good humour: with them, humorous, even slightly rude language will work best. It is a very different matter with oboists and bassoon-players: they have to blow into a narrow reed, and in such a manner that a great amount of air remains stored up in the chest to be released cautiously and gradually; this causes their blood to rise to the brain and makes them so nervy that one has to make one's remarks to them with the greatest possible tact. . . .

Remarks like this, and many others, could only be made by conductors who came 'from the ranks'. They had their experiences when they themselves were still playing. Nikisch had been first violinist in the Vienna Philharmonic.

As the famous *Kapellmeister* said, the conductor has to address different players in different ways. But we might also add that these variants must be hidden beneath an apparently completely equal treatment of all of them. Because independently of the particular susceptibilities characteristic of the players of certain instruments the musician also reacts according to his personal temperament. Thus, the almost morbid sensitivity of some horn-player might resemble the nerviness of Nikisch's oboist. Perhaps his tone would not be nearly so moving if his character were not so execrable.

Like a father who is careful not to arouse jealousy among his children, the conductor must avoid showing his preferences. It is one of his delicate tasks to 'know' how to deal with his musicians.

In his book, Professor Gosset warns never to make corrections in public. This is certainly the best way to manage those you are leading. But if the matter is easy for the surgeon whose operating activity is continuous, it is almost impossible for the conductor who has to interrupt all the time in order to make his remarks in front of all. It will be a question of 'the manner' in which he makes them . . . the trouble being that he has not always time to choose. In this respect, no one escapes *mea culpa*, the writer of these lines less than anyone else!

It has been said that the conductor should avoid idle talk. It is just as necessary to speak concisely but clearly. It is not enough to interrupt, to say: 'It's bad, start again'. He must say why it was bad, mention the errors, explain the causes and —most difficult problem—say how it ought to be done. Few succeed in solving the latter.

The *bâtonneurs* do not know how to express themselves in front of an orchestra, which is just as well because of the stupid things they might say. But many conductors—even good ones—do not always *dare* tell their musicians everything. Their pusillanimity will gradually grow into excessive tolerance towards the rank-and-file musicians and more so towards the soloists. They will almost limit their remarks to the string-players. A conductor can safely reprimand twelve second violins; the first oboist, however, might become very rebellious when singled out by an inferior conductor.

Union influence and even communist infiltration have often emboldened musicians to try to escape the tyranny of the conductor. A long time ago an excellent clarinettist came to me in the interval of a rehearsal and informed me he was unable to 'feel' the solo he had just played in the speed at which I had taken it. He asked me whether in such a case a conductor ought not to adopt the soloist's speed! To what would this lead? It is in this manner that the ancestors of my clarinettist had built up the false tradition of the deplorable *accelerando* in the prelude of the Prison Scene in *Faust*—and this despite all logic, and despite the fact that *a piacere* on the contrary means a slowing down only for the last few notes of the phrase. By the way, clarinettists sometimes do tend towards being voluble: another remarkable soloist whom I had asked not to rush a cadenza in the *Zampa* overture answered that this was how his master Turban had played it. To which I replied this was not the place to perpetuate mistakes, not even those of the masters! It is quite possible for conductor and player to hurt one another! How many of our excellent tympanists, for example, would consent to create a proper relation between their own *forte* and the proportionate tone-volume of the orchestra? Especially in the classical works where their tonics and dominants, doubled and sometimes trebled by trumpets and horns, really drown the melodic line. But on the other hand, how many conductors ask such things of their musicians?

The real conductor need never be afraid of those he conducts. But he must know how to command them without arrogance and how to convince them without hurting. He must also himself obey certain conditions essential to the task he has assigned himself. After a certain amount of hard and thorough work, for example, he must know exactly when to stop rehearsing, on that particular day. In music, as everywhere in life, one of the leader's essential duties consists in appreciating and acknowledging an effort. There is a moment where the conductor, even if he is not yet completely satisfied with the result, must stop himself from going on. On another occasion he might have to get his players to do some work which they fear and which they don't like doing.

Sure as a conductor has to be of what he says, he must also be ready to confess to an error of his own. With some wise reservations, he has even to take notice of the opinion of the mass of his subjects. This applies notably to the evaluation of the instrumentalists and particularly to that of the second soloists. Having only rare opportunities for showing their qualities, they are handicapped by the fortuitous conditions which make their performance necessary. A conductor might be afraid of entrusting them with a first part. But when the case does arise, they may show great mastery which only awaited the opportunity for showing itself. By way of contrast, the hazards of an audition may sometimes favour an instrumentalist who after a brilliant performance before the jury will reveal himself as only an average orchestral player.

In opera, the conductor's cowardice in front of the singer is even more pronounced. He thinks he is excused by pretending he 'has nothing to do with those people who know nothing about music'. But with this he confesses his guilt. If there are various ways of talking to players, there are others for dealing with singers. The former are generally full of good intentions, and demand nothing but to be conducted. They sin most frequently through the fault of the conductor abandoning them too much to their own ignorance.

The majority of singers, particularly operatic ones, make us think of an actor or a lecturer who expresses himself in a language he doesn't know. Their elementary knowledge of music is generally scant and sometimes nil. Often, their voice has been discovered too late to be properly trained. The latter applies to other countries as well as to France. I conducted *Tristan* in the original language with the collaboration of artists whose perfection made me gasp. They even sang immediately from memory the cuts which I gave them. Until then I had not thought it possible that Tristan and Kurwenal could reach and keep up such a speed at the end of the first scene of the last act and still maintain clear articulation. However, looking at the piano score the famous tenor had used for his studies at Bayreuth, I noticed that all the beats were marked in red pencil from one end of the score to the other!

An anecdote reports that another tenor—an Italian, this time—had an audition with Toscanini. The illustrious maestro accepted him, but said to the impresario: 'Don't let him learn anything about music, will you!'

Outside France, there is no need to fear that a singer would come on stage before having properly learned his rôle with the *répétiteur*. If there are errors he will be sent back to the studio to study his rôle properly. It is not the same in France, where the 'near enough' is more than just tolerated: it is permitted by director and conductor!

I remember a Marguerite in *Faust* who was so ignorant of her part that I had to tell her not to watch my right arm but my left hand, which I held open for long notes and closed for short ones, like a police-constable directing the traffic—and this throughout the whole performance!

You cannot then talk to these people who cannot read music, as you do to orchestral players so worthy of being called 'musicians', that beautiful word they so often make the mistake of detracting. Hans von Bülow once said: 'When the curtain is up, I can't enjoy myself any longer!' You must try to win the confidence of those spoilt children, the singers. Then they will really try to satisfy the conductor who knows how and dares to command them. Often they don't even know the cause of their success and believe more in the impression made by a pause than in the beauty of their voices. Once before the public, they who were so restive at rehearsals throw imploring glances at the conductor, quite out of the character of their respective rôles. You have to make them understand that, having learned their rôles really and properly and having followed the conductor's wish in the rehearsals, they will find themselves completely free, once on stage, from the necessity of having to take their eyes off their Isolde or Manon, in order to crave a 'saving' gesture from their tyrant. For this reason the real conductor has first to enforce rigorous studio work with the singers, and even to force them some-

F

times to take their eyes *off* him. Then he has to try to *prevent* himself from giving them their entries. Only thus will the *singing* stage fulfil its real meaning.

But in order to arrive at this state of affairs, one must first force the singers to know their parts perfectly. And this is still more difficult in France with those singers who are good musicians. Because the latter, through the very superiority they have over the others, are too indifferent and do not work hard enough.

A really good and easy-flowing performance requires that the singers—like a soloist in an orchestral concert—*seem* to be *followed* by the conductor. The latter, however, must previously have organised this impression. Then he will be able to, and *must* actually, in the moment of performance, give to those he conducts the feeling of being free from subjection.

During the interminable Marseilles episode of the French Radio, a Provençal grocer-woman who, like everyone else, was a black-marketeer, said to me: 'Generally speaking, we may consider ourselves only conditionally free!' In front of the conductor, singers, virtuosos, and soloists as well as certain stage directors should never be in anything more than 'well-supervised liberty'.

The same applies to the actor when dramatic art joins music. The conductor alone knows when they must be followed, and when led. The synchronization of a word with certain notes or chords will light an emotional spark of perhaps even greater intensity than in opera. The most remarkable example is the end of the dialogue between La Renaude and Balthasar in *L'Arlésienne*, when unison between word and music in the *Adagietto* is achieved by the complete coincidence between the word 'coeur' and the orchestra's *poco sforzando* which is so expressive.

Adagietto de l'Arlésienne

Eh! bien, alors, serre-moi bien fort   Voilà cinquante ans que je te le
sur ton cœur, mon brave homme.   dois, ce baiser d'amitié.

This striking example may suffice to indicate what subtle, patient and slow preparatory work must precede the manifestations of one of the most beautiful forms of art which is generally just improvised and left in the hands of indifferent *bâtonneurs*.

Nikisch was right. Among the indispensable gifts of a conductor the psychological sense plays an important part. But it would not be sufficient by itself. I have to think again of Professor Gosset's remarks about the speed of visual perception and about visual memory. At the same time, I remember how Toscanini—despite his legendary shortsightedness—noticed that a substitute had slipped into the Orchestre Straram which he conducted as guest—and refused to go on with the rehearsal unless the original player took his place again at the desk.

The conductor with bad eyesight is as handicapped as the one who cannot hear. The musicians must feel all the time that they can neither escape the eye nor the ear of whoever conducts them. The conductor must show them incessantly how keen is his own concentration on everything, notwithstanding his personal tastes and preferences. His musicians must feel that he will not abandon any of his demands, and that they may just as well give up any attempt at exhausting his patience. He himself will never allow them to quit before he is completely satisfied.

The conductor must no more neglect his own behaviour at work than tolerate indifference or nonchalance in front of him. If he arrives at his desk before all the musicians are at their places there will be no end of noise and shuffling. His authority must make itself felt even before he comes in, last of all, and amid general silence takes his place. If he notices that some player is absent or late in arriving, he must avoid giving in to his natural urge to make those who have arrived punctually feel his resentment.

He must react calmly but with courage against all attempts to relax discipline which culpable demagogy has favoured for some years. Among these, smoking at the desk is not the least of all the inadmissible licences. The best musicians might be reminded that they owe to their art the same respect which they accord to religion by abstaining from smoking in church. Once no one would have thought of doing so in a concert hall or theatre, and the fire brigade watched more scrupulously than today over the strict observation of police regulations.

Once, also, musicians used to tune their instruments before walking to their desks. I can still remember the deputy conductor of the Opéra standing at the bottom of the steps leading to the pit, tuning-fork in his hand, and making sure that *all* instruments, strings as well as wind instruments, were scrupulously in tune. Times have changed, indeed, and sometimes in a regrettable manner. It would be vain to advocate a sudden return to this excellent discipline, but one might perhaps induce musicians to be less careless by having the bell which rings to call them into the pit, tuned in A. This would then give them the correct pitch as they walk to their desks.

A lot could be said about behaviour in front of the audience, too, and conductors alone—and always—are responsible for it. Through the conductors' cowardice musicians have become careless when playing. They cross their legs and loll back in their chairs. Once, no one dared appear at an evening concert in anything but tail-coats. After the 1918 peace, circumstances were used as a pretext for descending from tails to the dinner-jacket. And as wardrobes will have been still more depleted by the last war, and as the cold justifies almost any sort of cloth-ing, we can imagine what efforts will be made to make orchestras gradually still more comfortable.

Finally there is one more point which we must mention because it influences a conductor's authority over his players. And since theatre directors are at least as powerful as conduc-tors, let a theatre director speak:

> Much is obtained by severity, and still more by kindness. But you can achieve still more than that by intelligence and impartial justice which does not take the individual person into account.
>
> Being director, I had to beware of two dangers which might have jeopardized my position. The first was my strong liking for people with talent—which might easily have induced me to show favourit-ism. I need not tell you what the second was because you have already guessed it. In our theatre there was no lack of young and pretty girls. I certainly felt myself very much attracted by some of them, and was given to understand that one would meet me half-way. But I took a firm hold of myself and said 'stop'! I was aware of my position and knew that it meant restraint on my part. Here I was not a private individual but the head of an establishment the success of which was more important than temporary, personal pleasure. If I had let myself go with some amorous intrigue, I would have been like a compass which cannot give direction be-cause there is another magnetic attraction working on its own.
>
> But from the fact that my conduct remained irreproachable, and that I always remained master of myself, I also remained master of the theatre and was never refused the respect without which there is no authority.
>
> You always have to distribute your favours fairly. Unless you do, you yourself will knock the support from under your own feet. Thus I directed the theatre for twenty-six years without allowing myself one weakness concerning actresses, although they would

have provided me with plenty of opportunities. But whoever has tasted the pleasure of governing will not lightly give up his position of strength by laying himself open to the reproach of favouritism.

This is how Goethe expressed himself in his conversations with Eckermann and Chancellor Mueller, remembering in his old age how, in his period of maturity, he was director of the Court Theatre at Weimar.

The older we grow, the more we risk being taken as examples by the young. It is important not to be a *bad* example!

VIII. TECHNIQUE

DURING one of the most barren periods of broadcasting, a programme called *Introduction to Music* made a welcome appearance and immediately gained public favour. The gentleman responsible for it had always held the opinion that at broadcasts as well as at concerts, the listener was never sufficiently informed about the meaning of the works he was going to hear. In addition, he was going to prove that the public could acquire a hidden taste for being taught something about music and orchestration.

Two persons conversed in an informal manner, one representing a tympanist of a great orchestra, and the other a young music-addict. This conversation pretended to take place before an orchestra rehearsal, the subject being the work to be played. A little later, after the supposed arrival of the other musicians, the rehearsal commenced, and the remarks of a *real* conductor were to confirm the kindly tympanist's teaching.

Then the supposed rehearsing started, and the *real* conductor, reading his script, said to the supposed orchestra: 'Well, today we're taking . . .' and he named an orchestral work. 'Give me the beginning. And be careful not to hurry the four quavers in the sixth bar.'

The orchestra then played and hurried the four quavers.

'Good'! said the conductor. 'Give me now the beginning of the *Andante*. Number 6. And be careful to do the *ritenuto* together!'

The orchestra started again and there was some unsteadiness at the *ritenuto*.

'Good!' repeated the conductor. 'Now give me . . .' and so forth.

From time to time, always asking to 'be given' this or that

passage well and truly, the conductor added in his funny accent: 'Vell, zis iss ze theme of vengeance, vich iss a contrapoint to ze theme of voluptiousness. Now yoo comprehend, n'est-ce pas? Ve vant only ze bassoon—immediately to hell vizz ze voluptiousness off ze clarinet!'

In the excellent intentions of this popular teaching, the inventor of this programme counted no doubt upon his conductor-dummy's summing up for revealing to the invisible audience 'how an orchestra works'. Partially he succeeded— as long as the superficial listener did not understand more than most of those regular rehearsal visitors. But for a professional, how many mistakes which could so easily have been put right revealed the bad routine of the majority of *bâtonneurs*!

For orchestral musicians, flowery analysis is generally unbearable. They react from it by simply treating the conductor as an empty chatterbox. As to its usefulness, let us turn to Nikisch's psychology. An admirer asked him once whether he ever explained to his musicians the abstract meaning of what they were playing. He simply replied: 'Would you explain to the piano-keys what one makes them play?'

As to the easily satisfied 'good' of the conductor, which was how he reacted upon every non-observance of his demands, one might think that his non-perception must have escaped the 'inventor' of the programme himself. This was really not the case. He only proved his willingness to share his dummy's, as so many other people's, contentment with the 'near enough'.

For a long time I had a copyist whose work made you think of those cashiers whose 'handwriting is so good'. His calligraphy, however, was spoilt by a certain indifference to musical accuracy. After some years of culpable forbearance on my part, I blamed him one day, being more nervy than usual, for his carelessness concerning dynamics, accents and slurs. His face suddenly lit up, and under the impact of this revelation, he declared: 'Oh! Now I understand! You insist that *everything* is exactly right!'

The basic quality of the conductor is to demand of others as well as of himself that 'everything is exactly right'. Two conditions are necessary for achieving it: *knowing* it and *daring* to show it. Alas, how rarely these two faculties are united!

We have already mentioned what devastations are due to short-sightedness, to long-sightedness, to double-vision, to colour-blindness, to astigmatism, to semi-paralysis, and even to quasi-blindness of the ears. Stricken with only the least of these complaints, how could a conductor correct and remove errors and mistakes which he has not heard or which he has heard as something quite different? He will never be able to demand that 'everything is just right', because he will never know when 'everything is just wrong'!

But there are others: those whose hearing is not impaired but who do not dare—or do not want—to ask for anything either from cowardice or laziness. Their number is legion! After stopping the orchestra in order to make a correction, they start again and will go on without stopping at the same passage even though the mistake may still persist. This will happen frequently as the players are always aware of this typical peculiarity among conductors. While being unafraid of exhorting the strings, they are cautious with the other instruments to the point of tolerance, and the soloists are almost certain never to be importuned. You can imagine what sort of a performance will result from this type of rehearsing! . . . .

During a crossing in an Italian luxury liner, a passenger rang for the steward and asked why her bath was so muddy. The steward said,

'Niente, Signora, solamente un poco di putredine'. . .

Isn't it the same when the brook of the 'Pastoral' Symphony or the waves of *La Mer* are polluted?

It is at the very moment when he thinks that something may be put off till the next rehearsal that the conductor ought to stop and to begin again.

The professional conscience and intelligence of conductors, their moral—or amoral—principles have been mentioned often enough in these pages. Let us now anticipate the future and let us imagine how television will add to the fantasy of our radio-music-teacher and how it will enable us also to *see* the conductor at work. Let us just watch him. Let us be objective. Let us forget everything about Metronomi and Commedianti, and about other *bâtonneurs*. First, let us think of the advice and examples he has been given during his period of learning, of his debut, of the closed circle of traditions in which he will have commenced his dervish-dance.

To begin with, he will have lifted his arms symmetrically— certainly—like all other pairs of arms he had previously seen. He will have beaten symmetrical beats in penguin-fashion, as people have always beaten, namely, unscientifically and not without pitfalls. From his elementary studies onwards, he will have learned good old Danhaüser's idea of how to beat 2, 3, and 4. In addition, he will have been informed that those modern times, the 'exceptions', the bars of 5 and 7, are formed by $2 + 3$ or $3 + 2$ beats, and $3 + 4$ or $4 + 3$ beats, respectively. This was the first error.

No one has ever thought of warning student-conductors against making more than one downbeat to the bar, beaten vertically. Such bars of 5 or 7, beaten in the habital manner of adding a $2/4$ to a $3/4$ or vice versa or of adding a $3/4$ to a $4/4$ or vice versa, as indicated above, will never represent a *genuine* uneven bar nor give to the ear the impression of actually being *genuine* uneven bars. This is partially also the composer's mistake if he marks them in this manner by splitting them up by a dotted *inner* bar-line. Only a little pondering is necessary in order to find the following manner of beating:

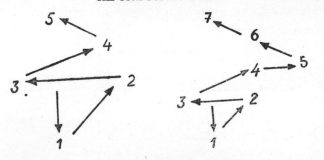

And this is not a complication but actually a simplification which does away with the confusing alternation of 3 + 2 and 2 + 3, or of 4 + 3 and 3 + 4. Ravel's *Daphnis and Chloë* offers examples of 'genuine' bars of 5 and 7, the natural rhythm of which is fatally compromised if the almost inevitable aid of a second down-beat is given:

Daphnis et Chloë de Ravel

In the manner of beating advocated above, the *horizontal* (light, not heavy) 3-beat inserted into the big 7/4 bars is very easy to beat and very *clear* for the players to understand. I had this idea on another occasion, when I began conducting long ago, at the 'first' performance (the real one) of *La Tragédie de Salomé*, in the Théâtre des Arts in 1908. Florent Schmitt's score was then written for only twenty players and did not sound less remarkable for it. When during the rehearsals we had *Danse des Eclairs* for the first time on the desks, the musicians passed ironical remarks about the 3½-4 time which at that period was a very daring innovation. But I stopped those smiles very energetically: 'This time is very easy, and I'll beat it like this.'

Tragédie de Salomé

This was in effect already a 7-time—a 7/8, in fact, but with the 'light' 3-beat then inserted at the end of the bar.

As a sequel to choreographic development since the times of the Diaghilev ballet, the fashion for 'dynamic' music was to result twenty years later in the dictatorship of the dancer who tried to impose his rhythm on the composer. The best composers have been busy experimenting with complicated rhythms which in many cases they might have been able to avoid. The conductors themselves had acquired a taste for exhibitions of acrobatics rather than for music. One of these specialists was the object of Messager's wise-crack: 'If this fellow can't find a 7/4 bar in the music, he'll make one up.'

Well before this period, I had received a useful warning from Chevillard. Having written down one of the themes of a symphonic poem with the interminable title *Pour le jour de la première neige au vieux Japon*, like this:

Pour le jour de la première neige au vieux Japon

I had not been aware that the frequent change of time at fast speed would prevent the musicians from correctly 'counting their rests' when they had nothing to play, and would make the conductor's task unnecessarily complicated. The cross-grained but kindly old fellow who conducted the Concerts Lamoureux, when accepting my score, had chided me for those perilous complications and asked me to alter them.

Which I did. Re-writing the incriminating passages, I simplified reading and execution by changing each irregular
group of three fast bars into one bar at moderate speed:

But in 1906 the innovation of this quaint mixture of 2 and 3
in the same bar was revolutionary, especially in the eyes of
Chevillard who told me one fine day: 'Look here, m'boy!
Your 8/8 bar is really 4/4. And I'll beat it in 4!' Which he did,
thus giving a feeling of double speed to the exotic theme of
which I had been so proud!

Since then, the use of these 'terno-binary' or 'bino-ternary'
bars has become generally accepted, and with many variants
as well. Personally, in order to facilitate reading, I have adopted the following sign for some of the groups of 3 :

El Greco

In the two preceding examples the subdividing of the
ternary groups is unnecessary, in contrast to *Daphnis* and
Salome. It is sufficient to beat the time as indicated by the single
figure placed at the right, and to shorten the duration of the
beat for the groups of 2.

Generally speaking, the conductor must avoid subdivisions.
They are too often applied at slow speed, in order to facilitate
a task which is too much for the conductor. He will make the
rhythm heavy by seeming to multiply the strong beats. Also,
this type of technique will slow down and sentimentalize the
music. In the rather rare cases in which 'subdividing' the beat

is justified, it must be done with subtlety and ease, but especially without beating half-speed.

An old theatre-conductor, under whom I played when young, had undertaken to write a guide on *Conducting*. I was able to take some intelligent hints from his work. But I specially remember one question he had asked me, answering it himself: 'Would you beat an *alla breve* in 4? I won't allow it!' And he was right. The abuse of 'subdividing' has deteriorated with the *bâtonneurs* to a mania which has even conquered jazz and the music-hall where the conductors, careless of the melodic line, conduct blues and foxtrot in an epileptic 4, caused by the insipid *ostinato* of the big drum. As far as 'symphonic' *bâtonneurs* are concerned, they will beat the Funeral March of the 'Eroica' in 4 from beginning to end, and the same in Agathe's aria in *Freischütz*, the string-syncopations of which then become simply unbearable.

Parallel with this tradition, there exists another of converting the quick beat of a lively 4/4 into *alla breve*. In the rich flower-garden of *graffiti* blossoms in the music library of the Radio, one may behold in the conductor's score of the Mozart *Requiem* that Metronomous has marked an *alla breve* for the fast 4/4 of the *Dies irae* and later, by way of contrast, a 4/4 for the slow *alla breve* of the *Tuba mirum*. Once logical, always logical!

Those poor fellows can't think further than their baton's end. For them, 'fast' means *alla breve*, and 'slow' 4/4. The cue given by the character of the piece, its rhythm, and its melodic line—what does it matter to them? It is much more serious than one might believe not to understand the slow and heavy march of the *Andante* of the 'Eroica', and to change it into a caricature like the clip-clopping of a procession of little funerals.

I was very young when, in the musical history course at the Conservatoire, good old Bourgault-Decoudray put us on guard against confusing ends and means; the means: time

(-beating), the ends: music and its rhythm. He added: 'You must wipe out the traces of time and bar-lines as a painter covers the lines of his sketch with colour. The music will remain.'

Beaten in 4, the Funeral March induces the players unconsciously to make ten little accents in the first four bars when there should be only one, at the beginning of the first bar, and half-a-one at the beginning of the third.

Beginning of the Funeral March ('Eroica')

Début de la Marche funèbre de la Symphonie héroïque
(appuis inconscients)

And meanwhile, who bothers about the most important element which is most difficult to play and to achieve correctly: the rhythmical polish of the anacrucis which precedes the first downbeat and later, the string triplets at the oboe theme? Here it is necessary for the conductor to 'count' himself, and also to demand and obtain the same from the musicians, for here, as in all similar cases, no gesture can replace the conscientious and special goodwill of every player. This is like Toscanini's 'triplet'-lesson in the Funeral March of *The Twilight of the Gods* which we mentioned in Chapter III. The remark of the master about lack of precision and inequality of tone-volume of the anacruces applies also in reference to the short and long values in their proportion of one to the other. The first three tones of the *Marseillaise* provide the best example. We may also add one from the second symphony by Saint-Saëns, at the beginning of the *Allegro*, at letter B.

Here it is necessary to watch that the quavers of the theme do not start too soon, *and also*, that they are not left too soon, especially when they are syncopated in the later course of the movement, at the *fugato* entries. The constant non-observance of this principle very often induces conductors to hurry unduly.

Besides, composers' marks sometimes are actually opposed (without the composers noticing) to the correct performance which they desire. Thus, towards the middle of the first piece of Debussy's *Iberia*, the short notes with dots are in danger of becoming less sonorous than the long ones with tenuto marks unless the conductor has worked *previously* at having the *dotted* notes themselves in fact stronger than the others:

Ibéria : Debussy

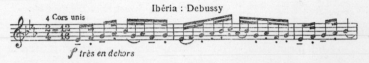

This treatment is the very simple applications of a trick always adopted by eminent piano-teachers, for achieving euqality of tone-volume. It consists of a preliminary exercise which stresses the short tones and especially those played by the weakest and most recalcitrant fingers, notably the fourth and fifth.

(Let us add that, when applying this method, the whole rhythm must temporarily change.)

Most errors are attributable to ineptitude and conceit, the latter always trying to conceal the former. One should rather limit than multiply the number of one's gestures. This limitation is characteristic of the masters, and the multiplicity, the resource of the feeble. Poor Commediante does not always know what to do with his arms. Therefore, in order to make himself interesting at all costs, he will 'subdivide' his beat, miming with his baton even the soloist's part during a concerto.

This same desire for a surfeit of gestures is responsible for the habit of beating empty beats and bars, which sometimes gives conductors the painful air of neurotics or of maniacs.

It is essential for the conductor to give an impression of ease. The players will assess him at his first gesture. To begin and to finish—or also to interrupt—is the touchstone of those who have taken up the baton. They must beat clearly and directly. They must know how to prevent their left arm from imitating the right arm, and must use it only for individual purposes. They must avoid 'clockwork' movements, that is, they must not move their elbows before their wrists and they must not move their wrists by rebounds. The wrist must not rise again independently after the hand has descended. This would prevent precision and only succeed in confusing the players. Finally, do not finish with a circular flourish, which likens a conductor's movements to those of a hairdresser.

The independence of the arms must always be strictly watched. The left arm has its individual rôle to play and must not repeat—except in exceedingly rare cases—the movement of the right arm. The actions of the left arm are reserved for the expression, not the 'time'. Its gestures are meant less for the ensemble than for underlining details.

Before finishing our advice on gesture, we must mention the 'natural' reflex of doubling up the body in order to achieve *piano*. Even the best fall for it instead of fighting the temptation, like any other unbecoming or ridiculous attitude.

The reverse of excessive slowness owing to the abuse of 'subdividing' is excessive speed, comparable to the driver who is exhilarated by the feeling of the accelerator's action under his foot. Excessive speed will often be the result of one of the gravest mistakes of the conductor: that of hurrying. This is one of the results of being a-rhythmic, which causes the values of the weak or semi-weak beats to be shortened. In a waltz, for example, the third beats will then be robbed of half of their real time-value.

G

If Schumann found that the playing of certain pianists re-
sembled the staggering of a drunken man, we may say that a
conductor who hurries gives the impression of having a club-
foot. And when he happens to conduct for a ballet, the dancers
give the impression of hopping all the time. Unconscious of
this mistake, the *bâtonneurs* so afflicted seldom succeed in
correcting it. Therefore they are a danger for their players,
getting them used to limping behind.

In a remarkable little book written by Felix von Weingartner, *On Conducting*, one can find the following succinct rule:
'No *Andante* must ever be so slow that its melody is not immediately recognizable. No *Allegro* must ever be so fast that
its melody is not immediately recognizable.' Let us take as
example Richard Strauss's *Don Juan*: the faster one takes it the
less clear it becomes. But if one knows how to play it simply
in time and properly 'articulated', it becomes clear and alert.

We have become too much accustomed to saying that there
are things which simply cannot be done, a particular example
being Wagner's figuration. This is often not true. The reason
is that the conductor occupies himself with those who don't
need him—the singers—and neglects those of whom he ought
to think in the first place. In the *Tannhäuser* overture, sixteen
bars after the first entry of the theme in B, in the *Allegro*, there
is no time to occupy oneself with the woodwind and the first
violins which continue the love-song, but rather to look after
the second violins and violas which *must* and *can* play their
arpeggios when allowed the time to do so.

Wagner: Overture *Tannhäuser*

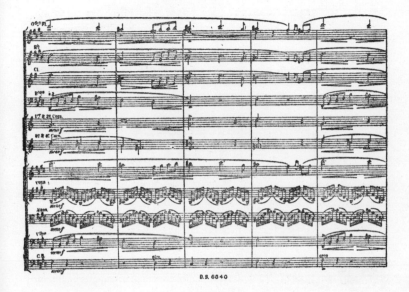

The same further on, at the return of the theme in E when in the sixteenth bar the figuration appears in triplets in the violas and 'celli.

The same again in *Till Eulenspiegel*, at No. 31. Is it really necessary to control the melody parts at the expense of those playing the figuration, and also eight bars further on, when the rôles are reversed?

Till Eulenspiegel de *Richard Strauss*

And still the same, in the course of the Minuet and the Finale of the sixth *Serenata Notturna* in D by Mozart, in order to allow the second violin solo to perform its passage, like the bass figure in the G Minor Symphony.

By way of contrast, in this Finale as in many others by

Mozart, and in some of his overtures, the conductor has to guard against losing speed as a consequence of the persistent difficulties of execution. Here indeed one must sometimes step on the accelerator. This procedure has to remain discreet and, of course, imperceptible for the listener. The right moment to do so is always the re-entry of the themes. Only after thirty-five years of conducting did I find at last the manner of playing 'lightly and in time' these Mozart Prestos. After having always endeavoured to achieve more precision of the beat, I was to discover that the only way to conserve speed is to weaken time-giving (means!) for the benefit of rhythm (end!). Having experimented with the Finale of the Symphony in D (without Minuet) No. 38, I forced myself to suppress the 'strong' beats. Having lightly marked the down-beat of the first bar, I let the orchestra go on for eight beats, hardly marking the first beats at all, and so forth as if it was one long bar of 4/1 which would be valid for the whole exposition of the theme.

Finale of Symphony in D by Mozart

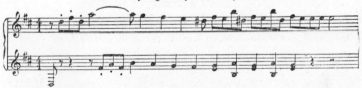

And so for the first time I succeeded in getting this piece in the manner in which I had always wanted to perform it! It goes without saying that experiments of this kind can only be made with the finest orchestras, and that for this experiment we presuppose preliminary work which consists in beating *all* the beats all the time.

Similarly, fast bars in 2 gain in lightness if beaten in 1, the same as fast bars in 3 may gain in lightness by beating 1. It is an error to insist on beating 2. Under the pretext of not shortening, one makes the music heavy. Excellent examples are Don Giovanni's aria in the first act ('Fin ch' han del vino'

—'Song, wine and women'), and Fauré's overture to *Masques et Bergamasques*. Also, moderate 3-time, as in the *Danse Macabre* about which we have already spoken (chap. III), should sometimes be beaten in 1 as well, whenever it is necessary to avoid too heavy accentuation in the accompaniment.

An excellent lesson in moderation, concerning achieved speed, is given in Dukas' *L'Apprenti Sorcier* with its continual regressions. These are seldom observed, and seldom, so to speak, scientifically established, owing to the approaching urge for acceleration—up to the sudden return to the *Lento* of the Introduction, at its precise speed, which conductors seldom succeed in finding again.

Once, in the course of a private record-recital, a funny experiment was tried: the metronomic divergences of various recordings of *L'Apprenti Sorcier* were compared. It was interesting to observe how in this strange steeplechase all the starters—despite their variants on the course—were in one bunch when passing the last *fortissimo* in F minor, owing to the fact that the composer's intention of speed must doubtless be so clear that not even the fastest runner would be able to exceed it. It was only to be regretted that this fastest one could not be compared with the slow-coach famous *Kapellmeister* who had been invited by Pierné as guest conductor of the Concerts de Châtelet whereas Pierné himself conducted in his place in the *Kapellmeister's* own country. The two colleagues both had put *L'Apprenti Sorcier* on their programmes. Now, after the French performance in the foreign country, the *Kapellmeister's* wife, who had not accompanied him to Paris, approached Pierné and asked: 'Is that then the real speed? But what will be my husband's reception in your country? He does not conduct it in 1, but in 3—from one end to the other! . . .'

The reason why the famous specialist of the Bach *Passions* and the 'Ninth' disdained to find out more about our music, has already been explained on a previous occasion, when I condensed it into the following lines: 'We have always held what the foreign conductors had to teach us about the works of their own countries in high esteem. Why do people in foreign countries decline to refer themselves to our conductors for French works?' (from the author's *Diabolus in Musica*, chap. 25). It is the same complacency which made one of our stars of the second magnitude say that in order to find the style of Wagner's works you ought to wipe out everything that came before him. With this, he meant to include French music as well! But this is not astounding at a period in which *ersatz*-manufacturers have *Pelléas* 'rediscovered' by young interpreters who have no more feeling for Debussy than for Messager!

This pretension at originality often conceals laziness or stupidity and often both. Eugène Delacroix wrote when only twenty-five: 'What makes a genius . . . are not new ideas, but being possessed by the one idea that the things said in the past have not been said sharply enough!' We should try to do things as well as our ancestors rather than try to do something *different*. The wish for innovating sometimes conceals the inability to do that which is necessary. This also explains the trend towards 'specialization', on harpsichord or viola, by pianists or violinists insufficiently competent in their own sphere.

> Above all, the conductor must be sincere towards the work he is going to perform, towards himself, and towards the public. When opening a score he must not think: 'Which interpretation of this work am I going to give?'—but: 'What did the composer want?' He must study the score very thoroughly indeed, so that while conducting it serves as aid for his memory, and not as an obstacle for his thoughts. His greatest triumph must be the beautiful performance of a beautiful work so that the ultimate success belongs to the composer.

This is again how Weingartner expressed it.

All errors become inexcusable in an age when wireless and

recording, consulted with discrimination, can mean constant teaching and control, despite the distance. Listening to a 'deferred' broadcast by the Orchestre National, recorded during the last rehearsal, I was able to hear once more what a pitiless mirror the gramophone is—just like the film.

Of course, I had been aware of the emotion and 'tension' of the players who by chance had found out that the performance was not a passing but a 'fixed' one. Fear of error may cause an error. Thus, a commercial studio allows ten times as much rehearsing for the recording of eighty minutes of music. In the case under review, however, very little of what was heard in this 'deferred' broadcast deserved preservation. Besides, serious technical shortcomings were revealed. Therefore, one ought not to use this radiophonic process without the greatest caution. But from a strictly musical point of view it was a completely unbiased eye-opener. There were things which neither can nor must be audible during the performance at the conductor's position. Besides, there was also the confirmation of imperfections which were to be expected, certainly, but not to such a flagrant degree.

In this way, I heard my orchestration of Albeniz's *Iberia*, done twenty years ago, but to which I now listened 'objectively' for the first time. Listening to my performance of Debussy's *Nocturnes* I surprised myself by saying, in *Nuages*: 'If I didn't know I myself was conducting I should say this is not in time!'—Which of my two egos was right? I could also listen objectively to *Sirènes*, my recording of which I had not heard previously, either. And in *Fêtes* there was again the impression of my young days, of a far-away mystery. The trumpet triplets, so difficult to obtain, and later those of the woodwind, at the beginning of the funeral-scene, were perfectly precise. But those of the little drum at its entry were hurried, as I had incessantly told the player.

Generally speaking, I had the distinct feeling that its usual precision of playing, so far from neutralizing it, enhanced the rare sensitivity of the Orchestre National.

You find in *Fêtes* one of the most striking examples of the subtle effects of the interpreter's personality, concerning the conscientious but not blind respect of the text. At No. 10, at the transition from *Animé* in 3 to *Modéré mais toujours trés rythmé* in 2, one must not give the impression of taking exactly half the initial speed which has accelerated from No. 2 and still unconsciously grown at the fifth bar from No. 9. The admirable funeral cortège, in order to preserve all its mystery, must then be taken at a little less than half the speed of the last *animato* bars preceding it. It may be 'imperceptibly' accelerated during its last four *forte* bars, in order to lead then to the resumption of the initial *Animé*, which should be exactly double the speed of *Modéré*. This was what Debussy wished, just as he never allowed the stupid, showy 'pause' before the cortège.

This subtle respect for the text was always advocated by those of the great masters who had also been great conductors. This is what Weber said:

> 'Time' must not be a tyrannic millstone which sometimes pushes you forward and sometimes holds you back. It must be to music what the pulse is to the human being.
> There is no slow tempo which does not demand in certain passages a faster speed in order to avoid exaggeration. There is no Presto, on the other hand, which does not also demand a slower treatment of certain passages in order not to jeopardize expression by rushing.

And then Weber adds to his 'saying' the following 'counter-saying':

> But for heaven's sake, the interpreter must not think that he is authorized by what I have said above, to adopt that foolishly presumptuous sort of interpretation which devours *ad libitum* any feeling for time. It gives the listener the same unbearably painful sensation as watching a bad comedian dislocating all his limbs. Animating or retarding of tempo must never give the impression

of shock, violence, or recoiling. Changing of tempo can only be effected in the musical-poetical sense over whole sections and phrases, in complete keeping with the passion of the expression. There is no way for a composer to mark this in music.

These are Weber's concluding words, added from fear—so he said—lest his counsel be misinterpreted. Wagner had the same doubts, too, when having written his remarks on interpretation, he added:

> A really serious warning: the greatest harm is done to the masterworks by performances which add arbitrary dynamics and fluctuations. This opens the door to the personal pleasure and fantasy of any conceited time-beater who aims at 'effect' and will lead us into perfect ignorance of all our classical literature of music.

We could continue quoting Schumann or Chopin or Berlioz, and all those musicians who served music. They always held up to contempt those who—already in those times —would have music serve *them*. Just as we shall always unmask those mountebanks who tell you that 'your knowing' can be replaced by 'your being known' if you are 'in the know'.

There being a contra for every pro, Wagner and Weber might surprise, nay, shock us by their interpretations of their own classical works. If only in our time, which has seen the realization of some Wellsian fantasies, we could explore the past and hear them by some process of anteriority-recording! But that is not important. Despite the contrast of tastes and ideas, we should always find ourselves in agreement with them! All of us would prove that we had honestly been working for the same goal. And honestly for the same ideal. We would prove, of course, that we had found after them and through them that what they had said had not been said sharply enough. That, emulating their august example, we had by no means taken our task too easily. And that, in truth, before appearing at the rehearsal, we had locked ourselves in with their scores which we were now performing in the proper manner, having preceded our work on the rostrum with plenty of homework.

'Except in very rare cases, don't improvise!' said Sainte-Beuve.

Everything that is well done, must be properly prepared and thought out. Demosthenes thought out in advance his speeches and prepared the beginning sentences. M. de Talleyrand worked out his *bon mots* in advance before the circumstances arose which brought them out as impromptus from him. If Bonaparte at his parades knew all soldiers by their names, it was because on the eve he had memorized them. It is all a comedy and has been rehearsed in advance.

No inspiration can ever replace rehearsal work. But how should a rehearsal be managed? It follows diverse traditions most of which are out of date.

In the first chapter of this book I have quoted the remarks which Liszt addressed in 1856 to the interpreters of his symphonic poems. In the first place he recommended the preparation of a full rehearsal by sectional rehearsals of the string, the woodwind, the brass, and the percussion sections. This was one of the most effective customs of long ago which has become almost superfluous. The quality of instrumentalists now is such that an entire rehearsal devoted to each separate group is unnecessary, with only a few exceptions.

I can remember the time when certain instrumentalists, such as the violas and double-basses, only very rarely possessed the virtuosity required for playing the works of Liszt and Wagner. I have always asked myself how the latter must have heard the Venusberg passages as executed by the violas of his period. And you can imagine his feelings if he heard the strings of today. You can imagine also the satisfaction of the old masters if they could have heard their scores played with so much ease by our contemporary orchestras.

The rehearsal scheme has thus been modified because of the development of the players' quality. It would be erroneous to hold up things by insisting on partial study by different groups for *entire* rehearsals. Also, another development, that of polyphonic writing, often changes problems. If you look again at the *Till Eulenspiegel* fragment reproduced on a previous page you will notice that the string passages which we then mentioned are also played by the woodwind. Therefore it would be advantageous to take the woodwind alone first, then the strings alone, and then those sections of both strings and woodwind together which play the same portions of the polyphony. This principle may even be applied to a number of classical scores such as Mozart and Bach.

One of the most widespread and most nefarious cases of negligence on the part of the conductor is leaving the question of 'bowing' to chance, and with wind instruments, even phrasing and respiration. A score will never come to full effect unless the bowing has been minutely regulated—and by a violinist, at that! The conductor who never played a string instrument in an orchestra must then stand aside and ask his leader to take over this long and tiring but indispensable work. Certain people, trying to find a pretext for rejecting it, pretend that the divergence of bowing gives the performance 'life', through the effect of the many different personalities! I never knew that multiplicity of personalities in disorder could result in anything else but in increasing the disorder.

Not only must the bowing be unified, but so also must certain fingerings, especially in the classical works. For in the days of the old masters, their contemporary executants did not possess the virtuosity of the musicians of today and did not like to risk high positions on their instruments. If one tries to have the Air from the Suite in D by Bach played with unified fingering and never exceeding the third position, this piece will have a serenity and pure sonority of which violinists have gradually robbed it—especially since an arrangement in 'C' was contrived in order to allow soloists to play the whole thing on the G-string!

Bowing has to be arranged so as not to break the melodic line any more than through the respiration of the wind instruments. The saving up and distribution of air on the part of the latter should give the impression of an organ. As far as the strings are concerned they should avoid interrupting the continuity of sound. They should give the impression that sound is being produced by an endless, circular bow. A bow is only a means and its dimensions are regulated by convention. The continuity of sound on changing the bow may be obtained by a pressure of the index finger on the bow when it is at its point: thus, the string players will be able to counteract the fact that while at its point, the contact of the bow with the string will be diminished by the weight of the arm working from the other end.

It has to be repeated again and again how much the conductor who does not 'come from the strings' finds himself handicapped. Even for fingering only limited freedom should be allowed, and even less so since catgut strings have come to be replaced by metal strings with their harder tone. Never again will we hear the velvety quality of the former string quartets, and today's violinists, like the young conductors, will never have known it! Since metal strings have come into use, the sound of the open string must be avoided more than before and the fingering has changed. One of my old desk colleagues explained the hissing string as follows: 'They say it's the strings' fault. No. It is the fingers' fault!' This is the exact truth, the more so as the use of high positions and of vibrato makes the fingers still less sure.

Will conductors and composers ever understand that in order to learn something about string-instruments it is not enough to look into books and treatises, or to have scraped a violin or a 'cello for a short time?

At the time of my colonial adventure about which I have

written elsewhere (see the author's *Diabolus in Musica*, chap. 27), one of the young people whom I had often foolishly trusted found himself baulked by my intention to resign. He duly went over to the enemy. But the adventurer-director, in the fear that replacing me might be too heavy a load for a beginner's shoulders, asked him if he felt up to conducting, for example, *Pelléas*. To which the ambitious young traitor answered: 'Certainly, because now I know all *his* tricks'.

You are bound to waste plenty of time if you imagine that greater experience is based on 'tricks'. The truth is much simpler. In the course of this book, for example, I make a special effort to discuss points which, despite their importance, are hardly ever discussed. For example: one always thinks of 'polishing' instrumental entries . . . this word 'to polish' has become detestable: the very fact of using it for one thing seems to imply that there are other things which do not need polishing—whereas simply *everything* ought to be polished! The same applies to the words 'meticulous care'. There is, of course, nothing in music which must not be treated with meticulous care! But let us return to our subject. It is not enough to begin the note on time, you must also leave it with precision. And rarely can people be bothered to do this. The 'life' of a rest is the opposite of the life of the note—this is too often forgotten. The rests are like the breath of music. They, too, must have their precise duration. But this has nothing whatever to do with the interruptions and the chopping caused by incorrect interpretation. There is only one way to give both the note and the rests their real value: to *count*—as we have mentioned above in another context.

If composers are in the habit of pushing their *forte* to extremes, how many interpreters are entirely unaware of how to give a rest its very important place in music? Too often we may compare musical performances to conversation without punctuation. Besides, the woodwinds' need for breathing, and the strings' need for change of bow, cause illogical interruptions and incorrect phrasing, comparable to the singers' untimely transformation of any literary punctuation when they have to breathe. And when the conductors take the time to watch over the strict execution of the value of the notes—which they don't often do—it is rare for them to be just as careful concerning the strict keeping of the rests. If they do think at all, they think of precise entries but not of precise interruptions—more difficult to achieve. While the sounds which ought to be sustained are often allowed to 'fade out', sounds which ought to be separated are not neatly defined one against the other. This neat definition of single sounds demands the players' special effort and incessant attention. The wind instruments must stop their breath and the string players immobilize their bows if they cannot lift them off the strings because the time is too short. Tenacity alone on the part of the conductor can achieve this constant diversity in the effort of his musicians, because even the best ones among them—and again among these, the ones with the best intentions—still have incessantly to be kept to the task by the conductor. If this procedure is adopted, the orchestral cake which so often remains doughy will 'rise', air will filter into the phrases, the music will 'breathe'. It is superfluous to give examples, for the listener—whether aware of it or not—will soon learn to distinguish between various types of performance—and he *will* notice!

Here it is the question, as we mentioned, of equal observance of the values of the notes and of the rests. The music-lover's auditory discomfort—unconscious and impossible to define—will be due to the performer's tendency to shorten weak beats or the weak portions of beats. This is what happens when the values of notes and rests are not properly kept. This tendency also explains the indispensable regimental big drum which punctuates the 'left-right, left-right' of marching soldiers. In addition, it is also the consequence of the non-observance of the rests, brought about by the fear of empty spaces. And this natural fear turns into panic in the frequent cases in which the whole musical flow must be interrupted for the length of whole beats which are part of the greatness of a work.

It can be said that, if the pedal-points are not always given their real length, the actual 'breaks' are almost never properly sustained. But if the performer 'has the nerve' to interrupt himself calmly and for precisely the intended length of time, he will achieve mastery, and the listener will feel the wings of the angel flying past. . . .

There is no secret, no 'trick' in all this. It is only the reasoned, critical observation of errors made in the past which we hope to escape in the future. For after each performance you must pass the examination of your own conscience, asking yourself whether you have faithfully served the composer. Often on the morning after a performance you may tell yourself 'how much better I should do it if I could do it again today!' Which does not alter the fact that *during* a performance you must never think of correcting yourself, but only of going straight ahead without 'listening back'. Because by 'listening back' you will only spoil what lies ahead of you. Only later can you examine and re-examine what you have done. It will prevent you from getting bored with some work because you will have the satisfaction of new discoveries.

In the Finale of Schumann's First Symphony, for example, the sequence which starts twenty-one bars after the recapitulation has a long *crescendo* from *piano* to *fortissimo*. From the instinctive tendency to become softer when a melodic line descends, and from the melodic context of the four-bar groups one has to forestall in the second part of each group the probable interruption of the *crescendo* which may deteriorate even further into a *diminuendo*.

First Symphony by Schumann, Finale.

Therefore you must, on the contrary, ask the instruments to utilize the descending portion of the melody for increasing the tone-volume. The power of the sequence will thus be increased. In the same way you must counteract a fading of the *crescendo* on the minims, therefore you have to ask for a special little exaggeration of the *crescendo* on the minims. The first movement of the 'Pastoral' Symphony by Beethoven contains another example, thirteen bars before the recapitulation. Finally, at the end of the 'Thunderstorm', one has to watch the reverse tendency which also is an instinctive one: generally, the tone-volume will increase on the octave-jumps. But the passage must be one extended *diminuendo*. Therefore, you have to ask for a weakening of tone on the *second* note of these octave-jumps. The thunderstorm's departure will be all the better for it.

Again similarly, in a string-unison, the tessitura of some instruments sometimes forces them to stop before the actual end of a phrase. Therefore you must take care that those who continue compensate for it by slightly augmenting their volume. This is the case in Fauré's *Requiem* when at the end of the *Agnus Dei* the violins have to abandon the violas and 'celli in the repetition of the initial phrase, particularly in view of the *crescendo* of the descending phrase.

H

Agnus Dei du Requiem : Fauré

You must also avoid allowing accents on the last note of a phrase which is *piano*, as *very frequently* happens. When there is a *diminuendo* one has to watch specially that the last note is even weaker, continuing the *diminuendo*.

All this is part of 'knowing what to ask for', the most essential virtue of a conductor. He must know how to deal with all sorts of musicians, because even the best conductors, the most famous ones, and the most popular ones, cannot always count on having a great orchestra at their disposal at all times. A good conductor often obtains unexpected results from a mediocre orchestra, just as a first-rate orchestra may become unrecognizable under the baton of a mediocre conductor. There are fewer bad orchestras than bad conductors.

Never let a mistake pass. But never forget to recognize those you may have committed yourself—the players will have noticed!

Let us mistrust our own special gifts of nature. Let us not multiply the tours-de-force of our early days. Space them out and ultimately suppress them.

'Learn' all the time, by watching your musicians. Then you can avoid blunders like this: a conductor who for a long time adorned the Opéra without ever being able to conduct more than three or four works asked the organ-player to be louder, telling him to 'pedal harder'.

Always think of making melodic phrases long without interrupting them by bar-lines or accentuations.

Take care that the players—strings as well as brass—after

putting on the mutes, do not play too *piano*, and after taking them off, not too *forte*, as they are inclined to do. The mute does not alter the dynamics but the tone-volume.

Following the same idea: the wind players, and the wood-wind in particular, uniformly believe that 'doubling'—marked *a due, a* 2—means an element of volume-increase whereas it is often the sign that a special quality is desired. In Rameau's suites we visualize the unison flutes as velvety, the unison oboes as hard, the piccolos as bucolic. Here oboes and bassoons are sometimes doubled, trebled or even quadrupled.

Coming back to the mute, let us draw attention to the fact that conductors sometimes fail to make sure that all the players have them and apply them. They must also make sure that *all* strings observe the *sul ponticello*, overcoming the strain this may produce upon their nerves.

Even during their early period of learning, young players should be trained by their teachers to watch these details of professional conscience. This is one of the reasons for the existence of the orchestral classes at the Conservatoire. They ought to prepare future orchestral musicians for their moral as well as for their artistic obligations.

Do not do things for *yourself* but for those who are going to listen. Therefore do not let percussion and brass thunder away.

'Cases when the brass should sound like a fanfare are few and far between.' That is how a young conductor of my acquaintance correctly expressed it—although he was among the less talented ones and although he was not afraid of asking in a Schumann symphony the brass to 'jazz it up a bit'.

Watch that cornet parts are not played on the trumpet (through sheer slovenliness). One generally neglects the particular character of this old breaker of hearts of the times when the 'Café-Concert' blossomed. In a brass *tutti* the cornet replaces the trumpet and forms the bridge between horns and trombones.

Before leaving the brass, let us mention again that the instruments whose tone-forming is slowest are generally placed far away from the conductor both in concert and opera. Therefore it is indispensable if you want to avoid their being late, that they should prepare in advance their tone-emission and breathe so as to play exactly with or even almost ahead of the beat. In addition, the horn players must be sure that their instruments actually point to the rear. It should also be possible in some—very rare—cases to make the horn player consent, like his colleagues in the Germanic countries, to 'lift' up his instrument while playing. Certain powerful effects will thus be magnificently enhanced.

We could go on *ad infinitum*. By advising, for example, conductors as well as composers not to lock themselves up exclusively with music. Painters and writers attend concerts much more frequently than musicians read or go to a museum. And it is well known how doctors love music. Among the precepts of Professor Gosset, does not this one apply to the conductor as well as to the surgeon?

'By watching others operate, you may learn what to do as well as what not to do.'

In his book, *Chirurgie, Chirurgiens*, the author did not neglect to deal in detail with operating theatres and with the best way of equipping them for the art of operating. In musical art this is a question which is generally dealt with arbitrarily by architects and indifferently by technicians.

Elsewhere I have mentioned how little some architects care to consult the ultimate users when constructing our theatres and concert halls. At the Opéra and Opéra-Comique, the practice-rooms for chorus and orchestra had to be allotted when the buildings were finished, and they are still partially unfit for use. Later, the Théâtre des Champs-Elysées and the Palais de Chaillot were erected with even less consideration for professional needs. Our concert halls are too small or too gigantic, and their platforms were built without ever consulting a conductor with reference to their normal dimensions and the appropriate grading of their tiers.

In our own day, and by a still inexplicable stroke of fate, a music-loving minister had the idea of founding the Orchestre National. A no less inexplicable stroke of fate decided that the musician put in charge of this project should take care that this was to be a perennial enterprise, despite the revolution threatened on account of it. Thanks to the financial resources of the State Radio, it has been possible to modify the platforms of the majority of Paris halls in which this nomadic orchestra carries out its activities while we are waiting for the Home of French Radio to be built.

Let us finish this chapter on technique with some musings on platform arrangement. Although they may seem to some to having nothing to do with music, they are very important for musicians who care. These ideas of concert halls are based on the best models as offered by the Amsterdam Concertgebouw and the Palais des Beaux-Arts in Brussels. It goes without saying that the distribution of performers and their numbers can be varied according to individual requirements and to the particular ideas of various conductors. For simplicity's sake, let us take for our plans the number of players and the distribution of the Orchestre National.

Fashion and snobbery have their influence upon this subject. Fot some years, certain orchestras have adopted a distribution according to which the 'celli take the place at the edge of the platform, formerly held by the second violins, to the right of the conductor. Some advocates of this reform argue that the bass line becomes clearer in this manner, especially for broadcasting. They forget that the said basses' tendency to predominate will thus decome accentuated. Besides, this arrangement which causes piling first and second violins into one group does away with the opposition effect which was the result of their former placing. It is also quite interesting to note that this specifically Germanic distribution happened to come into favour in France after the Liberation.

The orchestral arrangements as suggested in our schemes are not solely the results of personal taste, but of seeking reasonable homogeneity. If placing the basses at the left shows the influence of the piano keyboard, well then, the first violins should have been placed to the right and all other 'singing' instruments, too.

I have especially endeavoured to bring together as closely as possible those instruments which are most frequently called upon to 'lead' in harmony. Therefore: violas and second violins, so often the upper harmonic layer of accompaniments; 'celli, double-basses and even bassoons for the bass layer.

I have also brought together those instruments through which the transitions of tone-quality develop, viz.: the horns, which as often tie the woodwind to the brass as they tie the different brass groups with each other.

In the distribution with choirs one should remove tympani and percussion far away from them so that there is less distance between choir and conductor.

It must also be understood that the different dimensions of halls and platforms pose individual problems and create particular demands which often necessitate modifications of the ideal seating.

The architects of concert halls must be the only people still ignorant of the fact that the necessary seating of an orchestra demands an allowance of about eleven square feet per player. For a long time concert platforms and theatre pits reached these dimensions only in rare cases. During the last years, however, the fashion for gigantic structures has caused architects to err in the opposite direction. So we shall only try to show the manner of seating musicians based on the above-mentioned requirement of roughly eleven square feet for each player.

The string players need the necessary room to use the full length of the bow. On the other hand, the musicians must not sit too far away from each other. The wind instruments in particular often enjoy too much freedom of space owing to differences in the orchestration of the works on the programme. But often through the exaggerated depth of the tiers on which they are placed, they lose contact with one another. An orchestra must represent one single sonorous block.

We have to leave the controversies about sound-refraction by parabolic walls to the acoustic experts. This controversy did not worry the architects of the old Conservatoire or the Opéra. In these pages we shall stick to the most rational seating of the players, based on the most direct sound-production and on the principle of how to give them the freest view of the conductor.

The platform is about five feet higher than the audience. The strings occupy its front portions. The wind instruments—first wood-winds—then the brass, percussion and choir will range themselves on the tiers, in the shape of an amphitheatre or at least with the wings slightly curved in order to give them a clear view of the conductor.

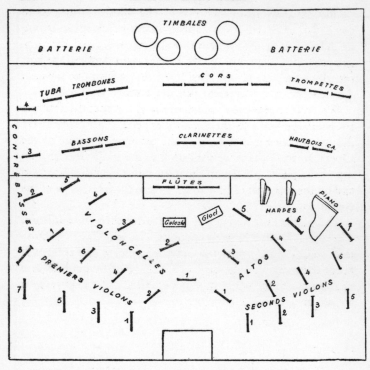

A: *Seating of the Orchestre National for performances without
choir. Provision for the organ varies with each hall. Generally, it is
behind the tympani (Conservatoire and Salle Gaveau), or at the
back at one side (Théâtre des Champs-Elysées and Salle Pleyel).*

This is the arrangement at the Concertgebouw and the
Palais des Beaux-Arts. But for us the main feature will be the
principle of practicability and dimensions, without interpreting 'dimensions' in some fantastic manner. Which means that
the tiers should have an elevation of slightly over one-and-a-
half feet and a depth of slightly under five feet—it stands to
reason that their width will vary according to the halls.

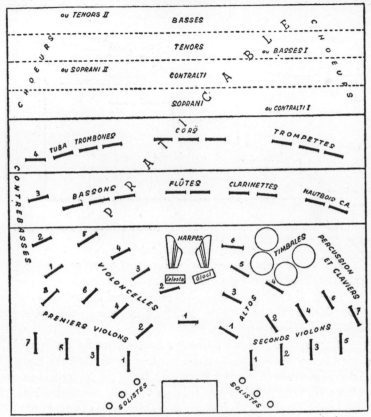

B: *Seating of the Orchestre National for performances with choir.
The soloists stand at the right and left side of the conductor, in front
of the orchestra. The announcer sits very far back near the control-
room. For performance of a work for orchestra alone, but with the
choir in position, movable steps should permit the bringing back of
tympani and percussion into their normal position over the brass.
See plan A and C.*

*Provision has also to be made for the organ, which will mostly be
found behind the harps or behind the percussion, at one side.*

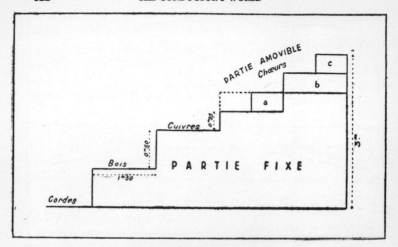

Section of movable steps

Plan A indicates the seating of the orchestra alone, plan B the seating of the orchestra with soloists and choir.

Plan C is a section of the movable steps and shows the way in which it allows a quick change from one to the other method of seating.

We may also consider a special little platform for the flutes (maximum of four) to be seated slightly lower than the first tier (wood-wind), placing them actually in the centre and in front of the first tier, in case of larger numbers of wood-wind and brass. The harps, in this case, should be moved to the right.

The measurements of the movable steps for the choir should be half the height and half the depth of the steps for the brass.

In order to get the right seating for tympani and percussion in the seating for performances without choir, it is sufficient to replace tier (a) by tier (b) and to leave out tier (c).

The movable steps have been indicated on the plans by horizontal lines, but it is obviously desirable that they should follow the curved line of desks. The same applies to the choir.

It has also to be kept in mind that the number of players

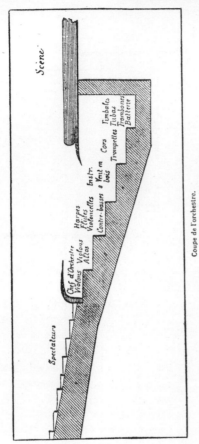

Orchestra Pit, Bayreuth. (1)

Coupe de l'orchestre.

must sometimes be augmented by one desk (viz., two players) each for every section of the strings, and that some scores demand four woodwind players in each section, and partially augmented brass.

We have still to discuss the seating of the orchestra in opera. In Wagner's memoirs we find many an interesting passage referring to it. And Lavignac's volume *Le Voyage Artistique à Bayreuth* gives the most ideal plan for the 'orchestra pit'. Our pits in France—with the Opéra being about the only exception—are almost always insufficient. Our directors are too fond of the financial return of their 'orchestra stalls' to sacrifice it to music. Because the theatre, of course, must not serve music, but music must serve the theatre. What do you call the people in the audience? Listeners? Oh no! Spectators!

But let us not complain too much! In his notes on *Tannhäuser*, we find the following lines by Richard Wagner:

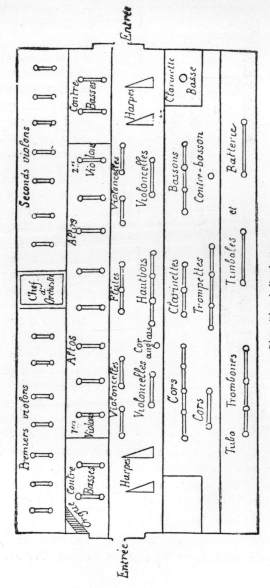

Disposition de l'orchestre

Seating of orchestra, Bayreuth. (2)

German orchestras generally have too few strings. Considering the urgent necessity for a good orchestral performance we should have lots of things to say about this lack of taste—and decisive ones, at that—in order to appreciate the state of affairs of music in Germany. But this would lead us too far astray. It is strange that the French, whose superficiality we so often decry, should employ a larger number of strings than often even the most famous Germany orchestras.

In the instrumentation of *Tannhäuser* I have tried to form a particularly powerful string section with such precise intention that I must insist that all theatres without exception increase their strings beyond their customary number. I wish my demands in this respect to be fulfilled in accordance with my rule. I declare that an orchestra which has not at least four good viola players to offer, cannot perform my music without murdering it.

And are we not equally astounded to read the following thoughts in Weingartner:

> Until now I have only spoken of concert- but not of *opera*-conducting. The latter is unfortunately not an happy subject.
>
> In the smaller towns you see four first violins in the orchestra, one double-bass, and one-and-one-half violas—because generally you can only half rely on one of them, a chorus of ten men and ten women, and tattered scenery and costumes. With this material they give *Fidelio, Freischütz, Magic Flute, Tannhäuser* and *Lohengrin*—and sometimes even the *Ring*.
>
> But even in the big opera houses, with better paid singers and a better orchestra, you can hardly notice any difference. Because too often a man without the slightest notion of art is at the head who manages the theatre like a financial establishment.
>
> In very few places is it recognized plainly that opera-management must be entrusted to an *artist*, viz., a *musician* at whose side (but not *above* him) there must be a council which, however, must have *no* say in artistic matters.

The seating of the players varies with the size of the pit. The ideal seating of Bayreuth cannot be reproduced anywhere else. Therefore one should at least try to achieve the indispensable contact between violas, second violins and 'celli on one side. and that of the horns with wood-wind and brass on the other,

For long years I have therefore personally adopted after numerous experiments—partially with Weingartner at the opening of the Théâtre des Champs-Elysées—the principle of massing the entire strings at the left, with the second violins overflowing to the right which is allotted to the other sections.

A certain colleague immediately declared this rational seating 'antiquated'. How far concern for fashion can go! Perhaps the gentleman was equally shocked by the antiquated way in which elderly people lay a table and dreamed of modernizing that, too. . . .

Let us add that especially in opera, you must endeavour to provide the strings with the opportunity for using the whole length of the bow which in their public-servant-indolence they are always inclined to neglect.

'Programme-building' depends on technique and psychology. Very few give it sufficient thought. Designing a programme is as difficult as designing a menu. The conductor may often be compared with the 'chef' who would mismanage a meal were he to serve the hors-d'oeuvre after the roast and the fish after the cheese. Every conductor will, in his first years, too easily incline towards multiplying his difficulites. Imagine, for example, that a young *bâtonneur* did not hesitate to put on the same programme the *Carnaval Romain* overture, Brahms' *Haydn-Variations*, Strauss' *Don Juan*, and Schmitt's *Psaume*.

It is important to know how to manage one's orchestra, the public, and oneself. For all three, effort must not be followed by effort. As the number of rehearsals is generally limited to three, it is possible to do sufficient work for a programme consisting exclusively of difficult works—especially in France, where the length of concerts is often excessive.

When letting yourself go with your taste for showy pieces you lose the consciousness of peril—and will risk the agonies of the sorcerer's apprentice. Thus your leave music far behind and adapt your ideal to that of Commediante.

IX. ACCOMPANYING

THE orchestral accompanist and the soloist often give the impression of two travellers together on a brief crossing who will never really get to know one another.

Accompanying depends on both the technique and the psychology of the conductor. According to his temperament he will be in sympathy with or indifferent or hostile to the soloist whom he mostly only 'puts up with' as the inevitable programme-attraction. For alas, such is the great majority of the public that it attends a concert less willingly when there is no soloist.

I remember one Sunday at the Concerts Pasdeloup when two young lovers, sitting too near for me to avoid seeing them, did not stop petting until the arrival of the soloist—after his performance they left, the attraction being over.

When hostile, the conductor does nothing to aid the soloist. When indifferent, he does not do enough. If he likes him, he might do too much. In the latter case he will, like the specialized pianist-accompanist, forego any orchestral preponderance whatever the requirements of a musical equilibrium. He will hurry his *tutti* just as the accompanist will rush the end of a song after the singer has stopped.

I have already mentioned (author's *Diabolus in Musica*, chap. 22) the erroneous conception of 'the accompaniment', that form of musical art which rarely receives the benefit of tact, intelligence, and musicianship which, however, it always requires. I have tried to explain the reasons by the bilateral prejudice which underlies this hidden conflict, and to analyse the different types of accompanying.

Finally, I recalled the memory of the ideal interpretation of Fauré's songs by Croiza and Cortot. Two artists of high stand-

ing had on this occasion met in such a communion of thought
and sensitivity that their very personalities had merged into
one: that of the magician of *Soir*.

We have always deplored the common error of so many
interpreters who superimpose on the works performed by
them what they call *their* personality—which can only be the
outward manifestation of their own taste. We said that the
interpreter's personality is a different matter altogether. The
interpreter's personality ought partially to consist of discovering the secret of the composer's intentions. These intentions
cannot be expressed in words. They are expressed in music.
The interpreter must find them simply by the rigorous but
intelligent observation of the text. This condition will be rarer
still if two artists share the responsibility of interpreting the
same work. This is the case when the conductor 'accompanies'
a soloist. Putting on one side the pianist who refused to
'standardize' the Schumann Concerto, or the violinist who
put his own accents into a Mozart concerto, we will only consider true artists who make up their minds loyally to merge
their efforts for one common aim. With these, contact is
generally easy. An Yves Nat, like a Gieseking or a Robert
Casadesus, won't ask for anything better than to 'standardize'
with us the Schumann Concerto. And a Jacques Thibaud,
Enesco, or Merckel will willingly repeat the phrase from the
the Mozart Andante in the correct manner of the preceding
orchestral exposition. Nevertheless, we have still sometimes
to reckon with certain personal peculiarities of first-rate interpreters who, while in complete agreement concerning Schumann, Beethoven, or Franck, may disagree on Mozart,
Chopin, or Debussy.

In addition, we also have the artist who once delighted us in
a certain work and who has gradually spoiled his perfect
performance owing to its frequent repetition. Thus, the admirable *Ballade* by Fauré may suffer a transformation of its
charming arabesques into virtuoso showmanship, owing to a

wrong tradition. This virtuosity is often easier than playing the piece at its correct moderate speed. For the virtuoso at the height of his career does not always stick to the indispensable daily practising.

Psychology, therefore, plays a considerable part in the relations between conductor and soloist. Technically speaking, accompanying puts some problems to the conductor to which he does not give sufficient thought and which he generally solves in a purely haphazard way.

The conductor bent upon giving innumerable masterworks their true shape may find accompanying a fascinating task. For this purpose he must consider his task as seriously and scrupulously when faced with a concerto as when conducting a symphony. Without the slightest modification of the composer's thoughts he must endeavour to interpret with complete subtlety the black notes on the white paper of the score. Like the *sforzandi* and accents of classical works, he will temper certain *fortes* of the 'accompaniment' such as the chords which punctuate the violin-solo passages of the second movement— *scherzando*—of Lalo's *Symphonie Espagnole* which too often roughen the melody. In chapter IV we have drawn attention to a traditional error of interpretation in the Finale of this work.

Whether we talk about instrumental soloists, about singers, or even about dancers, the conductor must always know when to follow and when to lead them. For those he accompanies are sometimes liable to drag, under the influence of fatigue or technical difficulties. It may also happen that out of a mutual feeling of respect, conductor and soloist (or singer), trying to follow each other, arrive at the exact reverse of their mutual good intentions. Besides, those accompanied by the conductor do not hear the orchestra directly, but we may say they hear it by refraction. Several distantly placed instruments may be quite inaudible for them, and at certain moments their acting may make them altogether deaf. Contrary to the majority of

I

soloists, the organist does not always hear himself, owing especially to errors of architects and organ-builders. In the Salle Pleyel, for example, neither the conductor nor the organist can and even *should not* hear the *piano* of the organ if it is to 'come over' to the audience as a nuance uniformly belonging to the orchestra. The organist having planned his stops to his satisfaction has often to modify them for this very reason, and even according to the difference of halls. He must more or less anticipate the beat according to the position of the organ or according to whether the transmission is electric or not. He has the most difficult task of all soloists.

For these different reasons certain soloists, and not lesser ones at that, sometimes ask the conductor to give them their entries in those very cases when the latter would rather feel inclined to efface himself in order to serve them in a very natural sort of artistic courtesy.

There are frequent cases when the soloist cannot hear—and even should not *try* to hear—his orchestral cues. Particularly at fast speed, trying to hear a cue causes slowing down or may even be responsible for 'gaps'. Especially in opera, it is wrong to inform the singers which instruments play their cues. But this is just one of the special vanities of certain producers who insist on interfering with the music.

The same conditions of indirect hearing of instruments apply to the orchestra players without their being aware of it. Therefore the conductor must watch that they never give in to the instinctive temptation of 'accompanying' a soloist 'by themselves' according to their own ideas—especially when the soloist performs a work well known to them. They must follow with their *eyes* and not their *ears* if they want 'to help the conductor'. The latter, especially in opera, can never insist enough that he and he alone is accompanying, and demand absolute obedience to his beat. There is only one way of succeeding: for a conductor to reduce his gestures to the indispensable minimum. We are here coming back to the excessive gestures of which we have spoken before, when we compared the orchestral conductor's gestures with those of the chorus-master and the church choir-master. We said then that it might not be a bad idea sometimes for an orchestral conductor to adapt his gestures more to those of the choir- and chorus-masters.

The custom of beating empty beats and bars in operatic works or accompaniments has always appeared to me unnecessary and even bad. Watching the great masters, notably Arthur Nikisch, I felt certain about it. It would seem quite natural that the conductor should act in the manner of the piano-accompanist who feels no need for beating or even for counting empty beats. Of course, the conductor has to think of his players, but it is sufficient to tell them that he won't beat. It is certainly natural for everyone to have his own particular way of doing things, but I am sure that mine has never yet led to accidents. It forces the players to be attentive and awake and gives the whole performance as well as the most unimportant recitative an atmosphere of lightness and an impression of ease.

Doubtlessly, this presupposes sufficient time for rehearsing— a factor which is too often neglected. But with sufficient rehearsing conductors and soloists won't give the impression of which we spoke at the beginning of this chapter, but that of a true collaboration. Many a masterwork of music the beauty of which is so often jeopardized by repertoire-routine will profit from this. The miracle of Fauré's *Soir*, preformed with such complete oneness by Croiza and Cortot, ought not to be such a great exception!

X. 'FROM MEMORY'

In one of his articles in *Le Figaro*, Reynaldo Hahn observed that for some years almost all conductors have suddenly and miraculously found themselves gifted with an extraordinary memory. It seemed that they had not even suspected themselves until the moment when Toscanini conducted without score. Then, emulating him, fashion dictated that everyone else should do the same.

The conductors of the great age never felt the need to establish the *means* as an *end*. They did not feel that they must conduct this or that score from memory. However, their minor colleagues of today think it is dishonourable if they do not ostentatiously push away the desk which the Bülows, Richters, Nikischs and Mucks never disdained. And unfortunately the public is too often taken in by the spectacular affectation of those who take advantage of what is simply a natural gift to satisfy their stupid vanity. I have spoken about it before (author's *Diabolus in Musica*, chapter 4). I have also mentioned that Toscanini's prodigious memory, certainly in part a result of his almost complete blindness, is even for him nothing but a *means*, and that quite apart from it, his genius consists in the unique musical organization of his mind and in the purity of his evangelical soul.

Orchestral musicians know only too well that the conductor who forces himself to conduct from memory risks spreading terror. One player who is an exceptional mixture of intelligence and professional integrity told me that he finds it impossible to resist the temptation of behaving as if, after a long rest, he is 'coming in' two or three bars too soon whenever the conductor feels like working his stunt. Immediately the acrobat—who, however, unfortunately does not even risk his life

—will become nervy and insecure. Then he will give an entry to the right which actually is due on the left, he will stretch out his imperious left fist to the trombones—who have nothing at all to play at this particular moment. He never looks at his players *before* the entries, but always *afterwards*!

Being given to such clown-stunts, these mountebanks know only too well that they have nothing to fear from a good orchestra which will fish them out whenever they have fallen into the water. For there is no conductor, even among the greatest, who has not been saved occasionally by the intelligence and cool-headedness of those he conducts. The conductors themselves know how to acknowledge it, and Weingartner has very clearly expressed himself on this issue:

I have still to analyse several points—firstly, conducting from memory.

This enormously impresses the publc. I myself am not given to to over-estimating it. In my opinion, a conductor may really know a work from memory. But he must always fear lest his memory play a trick on him, either as a consequence of understandable emotion, or by reason of any other disturbance. In this case it is always better to have the score on the desk, because after all there is a public which wants to enjoy the work and not to admire the conductor's memory. I recommend disregarding the score only on such occasions when a conductor is so much master of a work that reading would be a hindrance rather than an aid; in other words, when the conductor, even though he may have started to read, continues to conduct from memory because reading handicaps him. It is then that the French apply the nice expression 'conducting by heart'. But this is a purely personal need, an individual habit which has nothing to do with the quality of a performance. If the conductor is so much tied to the score that he cannot take his eyes off it in order to look at the players, he is only a time-beater and an ignoramus who has no claim to being called an artist. Conducting from memory and affecting a virtuoso-attitude is anti-artistic, because it means that a conductor tries to attract attention to himself which ought to be centred upon the work. Sometimes one may watch a conductor putting the score on the desk *although* he conducts from memory, for the simple purpose of not attracting attention. This is an attitude of complete integrity. But on the whole I think it is entirely a matter for the conductor himself and for no one else whether he wants to use the score or not. A good performance, conducted from the score, is valuable. A bad one, conducted from memory, is not!

There are many contradictions in the caprices of memory. Certain scores seem to be ever fixed in our minds. We may conduct them even after very long interruptions and again rehearse them almost without having read them beforehand. In other scores, some 'gaps' remain, a few bars here and there ... although we read and conduct them again and again. Shall we rob ourselves of the opportunity of throwing an occasional glance at some passage or another, during the performance? This gesture of the conductor is entirely warranted—unless he does it in a way which reminds us of some duty officer thumbing the dog-eared pages of a report. The best criterion for absolute knowledge of a score perhaps is whether a conductor can turn the pages 'from memory'. But once again: why do it, when the issue is not to give an exhibition of mnemotechnical prowess, but a good musical interpretation? Yes—but alas, whether conducting from memory or not, many conductors have an idea of interpretation which has nothing to do with music, anyway.

We have already said that their preoccupations are frequently mathematical, and that their scores are overloaded with *graffiti* which look like a cook's household account or a sick person's temperature chart.

$$\frac{2}{4} \text{— 1. 2. 3. 4. 5. } \frac{9}{8} \text{— 1. 2. 3. } \frac{4}{4} \text{— 2.}$$

This fixes in their minds the fact that there are five successive bars of 2/4, then two bars of three beats each, and two of four beats each. The lines you may find drawn from the violins up to the flute, then down to the violas after passing the trombones, indicates successive entries the conductor intends to give—if possible—to the instruments. And the principal dynamics are reinforced with a thick red or blue pencil. No question here of melody or harmony, of course. Conductors of this kind do not read the polyphony any more when conducting from the score than they understand it when conducting, so to speak, 'from memory'. They follow either with their eyes or with their memory a sort of district road-map which has nothing whatsoever to do with music—which is, in fact, further distant from music than the public will ever suspect! This sort of procedure ought to be banished. It is all the time the melodic, rhythmic and polyphonic texture in the head of the conductor which ought to dictate the movements of his arm. Even in the case of a succession of equal bars or similar formulae—must they really be 'counted' in order to be conducted properly, if the score is really *known* by the conductor?

Certain conductors cannot visualize a *tempo* except by its mathematical relation to the metronome. This reference—a medium between composer and conductor which may have its use when a conductor studies his score at home, away from the orchestra—interferes with actual music as if one were measuring it by the yard. In the course of a *rallentando* or an *accelerando* between one speed and the next speed, the metronome-maniac will 'inscribe for his use' intermediate metronomical figures. He is incapable of feeling by himself the natural progression of the rhythm of a phrase.

It might be supposed that the majority of these conductors are simply without musical talent. This is sometimes correct. But it is sadder still to realize that they are lazy, or simply careerists. Our profession is at a crisis of ethics even more than at a crisis of quality. This applies not only to the country of Berlioz but also to that of Wagner. It seems that growing orchestral costs induce conductors more and more to improvise their performances. Was it not quoted in a conversation about one of our most famous French conductors as one of his major exploits that at Salzburg he had mounted a *difficult* programme of French music with the Vienna Philharmonic, with only two rehearsals? What a rich idea one must have over there of our professional conscience! But then it happened here in Paris, too: did not the doyen of *Gastdirigenten* outbid his French colleague by 'mounting' two Beethoven festivals with one single rehearsal? 'We know all this music so well—so does he!' was the explanation of some unscrupulous players.

'Oh, the brave men!' exclaimed the conqueror of the Reichshoffen cuirassiers. We might reverse it, and musicians of integrity should rather say with reference to conductors who so blatantly neglect their work: 'Of all the dishonest people!' One speaks too easily of certain of these conductors as 'great workers'. This is not so. They are simply bad workers because they want to get too much done in too short a time. And when one day they want to change things—which is rare— they cannot because through working too fast they have forgotten how to work well.

Less and less can one see the fundamental qualities in orchestral conductors. Artistic devaluation has made the most famous orchestras accessible to the most mediocre timebeaters. This is how by dint of the ancient halo of the *Kapellmeister* the most inconceivable specimens can be sent over from abroad to France, often for reasons which have nothing to do with music. With the help of politics, any *bâtonneur* has only to announce his desire of conducting here, and the best orchestras will be put at his disposal.

It must be said that the public is to a considerable degree responsible for this sad state of affairs. Too often it looks at the conductor rather than listens to him. His exterior effect being beyond doubt, he persuades the uncertain audience with his cheap gesticulations that the hawkers' goods he sells are of real gold. But alas, must not even the sincerest conductor sometimes deceive the publc—not by the quality of his performance but by his choice of works? For it is not true that even the 'freest' of conductors can only play what he wants and what he loves. Like all other interpreters, he plays certain works by choice (good or bad), others from a sense of duty, and others again, by obligation. Nevertheless you should not commit yourself to certain works—any more than to certain people! Let us come back to the exterior effect of the conductor upon his public. We have said that not only does it exist, but that it is almost obligatory. Certain great masters sometimes disconcerted their public by remaining, as far as could be seen, almost outwardly impassive—the influence of a mere glance is enough for the orchestra which at certain moments does not need anything else from the conductor. Once again let us quote Weingartner, whose sobriety of gestures was legendary:

> Many *Kapellmeisters* have been criticized for making too many movements. There is some truth in it, for the mechanical aspect of conducting is not at all beautiful in itself. And the figure in black tails, armed with a baton, may appear ridiculous if the arm sweeps around instead of directing, and if the body in the exuberance of sentiment is contorted from right to left. But an ungenuine calmness and a spurious pose are equally repulsive. There are, thank heaven, moments in music where you have to move if you want to conduct, unless you have no blood in your veins. Therefore an excess of movements is always preferable to the reverse extreme, because it is, at least generally speaking, a proof of temperament without which there cannot be any art. One should not poke fun at a young conductor full of talent who is as yet unable to control his passion, but simply advise him in a kindly manner to keep his body still and to try *not to make more movements than are absolutely necessary*. The expression of each passage will then indicate the correspondingly larger or smaller baton movement, Certainly, a perfect harmony between movement and achieved effect can only be acquired gradually.

In the first place, the public is impressed by purely physical appearance. A short conductor will be handicapped and will

not always be able to compensate by his professional value
the disadvantage of nature. Conversely, the tall conductor
with a slim figure is favoured by the gods. If he knows how
to adopt the grave profundity of the *Generalmusikdirektor* and
the distant scowl that seems to go with it, he can almost allow
himself not to be much of a musician. A certain elegance is a
'must' for these two types whereas a certain easy-going air
suits those whose conspicuous circumference allows even
corkscrew trousers. They point to 'a worthy type, a man who
thinks of nothing else but his music'!

Certainly the conductor does not escape moods of fashion.
For some years now they've been 'playing Toscaninis' in our
noisy brotherhood!

By a sort of poetic justice, radio is fatal to charlatans. Gym-
nastic efforts and baton-histrionics do not go beyond the
studio walls and do not affect the invisible and innumerable
audience which judges the conductor. There is even no reason
to worry about certain exchanges of artists or certain missions
sent to foreign countries which frequently are due to some
special interests, and which too often risk rendering bad
service to general good and especially to national reputation.
With a simple studio broadcast, artists go every day on tour
to distant countries, and there are no frontiers. The microphone confers upon listeners the sensitivity of touch and hearing of the blind. The wireless listener can recognize an
orchestra and a conductor before the announcer has named
them. Better still, he hears how the same orchestra sounds
under a different conductor. From afar, he can compare and
judge. He does not take for granted any of the things represented as great achievements by mere publicity or routine
of the press.

Very soon television will allow us to entertain the public
with the following retrospective sketch: A conductor will
conduct the *Tannhäuser* overture, with his gestures limited to a
minimum. Then it will be announced that for the impending

second performance the orchestra will not look at the conductor! And under these conditions the conductor will be able to demonstrate how this piece was once 'played' by the baton-virtuosos. Then he will juggle with the violins, and he will tickle the violas, he will exhort the woodwinds, stare at the Venusberg tambourins and box with the trombones. And in the paroxism of the ending *tutti*, his outstretched arms will stress the traditional horn-blast of which Wagner probably never dreamed.

XI. THE CHORUS-MASTER

EVEN more than the telephone, the wireless has changed the relationship of time and space between people.

Hitherto it has only been possible for amateurs and for sufficiently wealthy musicians to go to Bayreuth, Vienna, Salzburg, or Rome. Now all of us can simply turn a knob in order to open our mental doors to the ghosts of Wagner, Mozart, or Palestrina. Thus we have been able for some years to hear all over Europe the chorales hitherto most inaccessible to the profane: those of the Roman basilicas—the Sistina and the Lateran chapels, etc.—united for a concert of works by the great Italian polyphonic writers of the sixteenth century.

Once more the habitual poorness of French choirs stand accused! This is a sad subject which I have mentioned before (author's *Diabolus in Musica*, chapter 19), and to which experiences force me sometimes to return. This accusation was to be confirmed again a short time afterwards in the course of a performance of Verdi's *Requiem* at the Opéra, a confirmation which was once more renewed on the occasion of the performances in Paris by the Leipzig St Thomas Choir.

The invisible Romans had made us marvel at the tragic *sforzandi* of their basses in Vittoria's *Tenebrae* and at the absolute *piano* of the tenors in the high tessitura of Palestrina's *Credo* or *Missa Papae Marcelli*. It was also marvellous to hear how little boys and young students thought nothing of the difficulties claimed as insuperable by our choirs, of singing unaccompanied with flawless correctness the great *Motet* for double choir by Bach which the remote predecessors of these Italian choirs had revealed to Mozart in 1789.

In France we have got used to pocketing such challenges without making the slightest attempt at reacting. For face-saving purposes we generally extricate ourselves by saying that there are no 'voices' in France.

We have to agree that especially low voices are more characteristic of Italy and Russia. But we ignore the rigorous eliminating test to which applicants must submit in foreign choirs, and the special exercises they are forced to practise for keeping up, conserving, and even for improving the voice. At all times some French singers have by intelligent work succeeded, either alone or with the help of teachers, in increasing their range at the bottom or the top register, and even to establishing a vocal quality which at the beginning was uncertain. It is known, besides, that certain regions of France, especially in the South, simply 'breed' voices. Therefore it is completely wrong—and unjust—to attribute the poor quality of French choral singing to a dearth of voices. We could have plenty of good singers in France, and choirs capable of rivalling in quality the best foreign groups.

The truth is that we suffer from a dearth of real vocal teachers for our singers and of real chorus-masters. Or, more precisely, we have too many of these 'teachers' and 'masters' who shamelessly parade some title which conductors out of cowardice and incompetence dare not challenge.

If there are some essential qualities which are indispensable both for conductor and chorus-master, the latter must also possess some virtues peculiar to his own profession. Choral art demands more patience, and preparatory studies last longer and are more laborious. Musicians who in their young days endeavoured to achieve ease of writing by learning their art slowly, will remember the fastidious 'six tests' applied by their masters while correcting their homework in harmony and counterpoint. They isolated all possible groups of two, viz.: Soprano-Alto, Soprano-Tenor, Soprano-Bass, Alto-Tenor, Alto-Bass, and Tenor-Bass. How many mistakes revealed themselves, forcing the student to start again the work which he had fondly believed to be complete! A similar 'polish and re-polish' is necessary for the chorus-master to assure correct rhythm before he can think of interpretation. Whereas the conductor must mostly try to single out not one or the other 'part', but one or the other *instrument*, the chorus-master's first duty is to merge all singers' personalities into anonymity. In a little treatise on sacred polyphony, by the choir-master of the Dijon Cathedral, we read the following definition:

> Sacred polyphony is a collective prayer offered by distinct persons represented by the lines of vocal parts, in other words, the 'voices'. Every one of them must jealously guard its autonomy but must abstain from any individual tendency at predominance over the others. The expressive power of this polyphony lies neither in wise gradations of *crescendo* and *diminuendo*, nor in more or less frequent speed-modifications, but in the characteristic activity appropriate to each part.
>
> The effect desired by the composer is entirely and essentially decorative. It excludes detail—not of preparation of each part by itself, but detail of ensemble!
>
> Summing up, the collective prayer of sacred polyphony will not be worthy of the sanctuary unless each vocal part, completely sure of itself, is able to 'come in' with perfect assurance, to maintain itself with firmness, and to produce musical sounds which are correct, firm, alive, which are ready to surrender to the choral ensemble without predominance, and which are ready to accept a rigorous and incessant discipline.

This principle of 'collective prayer' could be adapted to all choral music, whether sacred or profane. It is really a question of making the individual *voices* anonymous in the service of the autonomy of the *parts*. But its application is more difficult in France than anywhere else. We are given to individualism . . . to a crazy extent on the part of the majority of our choristers. And we must also consider how little attraction professional chorus-conductors find in their art, in France. In Italy as well as in Germany or in Russia, these chorus-masters are real specialists with knowledge of voice and singing. They

feel that they have achieved an aim when they have the
honour of being put at the head of a choral society. In France,
the chorus-master generally has the ambition of becoming an
orchestral conductor, whether he has the necessary qualifications for it or not. He just does his work as a necessity unworthy
of him, with the one purpose in mind—to conduct an orchestra—and when he succeeds in doing so, he will mostly do it
just as badly.

Under this sort of direction, the best foreign groups would
not make any better showing than the French ones. Conversely, our Paris choristers, some two hundred of them, can
sometimes show unsuspected qualities when conducted by a
musician who has a flair for choral art. The public generally is
ignorant of the fact that Paris has not more than two hundred
real choristers. One finds them grouped under the different
banners of too numerous choral societies and under different
batons, with variable qualities of execution which irrefutably
affirm that it is the conductor who makes all the difference.

We have to dwell on this point, too. In France, so little
importance is accorded to the conductor—whether of choir
or orchestra—that it was once said that a great manager—a
really great one—had made the following wise-crack, after a
dispute with his orchestral conductor: 'Let him resign . . . I
shall let someone else conduct—it doesn't matter whom—the
concierge will do!' But the conductor did not resign. Whereas
at a later period an unworthy successor of the great manager
appeared indeed to have really called a concierge to the conductor's desk.

'Truth is so near the caricature of truth that it is not surprising they are sometimes confused', wrote Eugène Delacroix. Therefore, the public seldom distinguishes between
good and bad . . . or mediocre . . . whether it is a question of
conductors or entire companies. Thus, the public seems to
have forgotten the marvellous pre-war Russian choirs, magnificently introduced by Diaghilev, since it made no protest

against the unworthy *ersatz*, offered by refugee groups. The latter were, of course, very respectable but should have stuck to driving their taxis or selling pickled cucumbers for their livelihood. One thought only of the quality of the Russian voice, of its flavour and its charm—without ever calculating how precarious their knowledge of music might be. It was just barely acknowledged that our own professionals were perhaps preferable in the repertoire works—but when it came to Russian music, that must only be sung by *these* Russians!

However, it was the same old tale as with those marvellous singers of whom it is said, 'maybe they really don't sing comic opera so well, but you should hear how *splendid* they are in operetta!' The fact is, they can't sing. That's all about it. They have only a beautiful voice. And that is not enough.

We have to repeat again and again: the main reason for unsatisfactory choral singing in France is the dearth of choral conductors. Let the latter be more competent and make higher demands—and choristers who have learned how to sing from quacks will soon be eliminated. Let them make higher demands not only on their singers but also on the orchestras with which they are to collaborate. Let them be less 'accommodating' with the orchestras and let them not, in the attempt to 'bring off' a concert, compete with each other in reducing the number of rehearsals to an absurd minimum.

With the financial means at its disposal, the radio could have brought about a revival of choral singing in France. But the condition would be a reduction instead of an increase in performances, and an increase in the number of sectional rehearsals.

In our age of haste and economic restrictions which Keyserling, the sage, called the age of the chauffeur, our conductors' greatest fear should be that they may not know any longer how to work slowly when they are given the opportunity. They must seek this opportunity and even courageously ask for it—

with the managements which are of course inclined to refuse it and even to fight against an ideal such as this.

Twenty years ago a young conductor, preparing a performance of *Freischütz*, told his orchestra during the *second* rehearsal: 'After the interval, we'll "touch up" the overture a little, and that will do!' Today, too, the conductors, overwhelmed by duties and honours heaped upon them and tired out by their conceited desire to be seen everywhere, do not *know* any longer how to make use of slow work for accomplishing too numerous 'touch ups'.

Culture, observation and perception are as indispensable for the conductor as his professional gifts. It is not enough simply to tell those you conduct that they are wrong, but you have to tell them why, and what to do about it, in order correctly to interpret the composers' ideas—even if the composers, as occurs frequently, have not written them down very precisely. The more we conduct a score, the more we *believe* we know it, the more difficult we are bound to find it. After a concert, one work will persist in haunting us. This will have been the best or perhaps the one work whose secret we came nearest to solving. This will be the work the study of which we ought to resume with the greatest patience and ardour.

But let us come back to the chorus-master and mention, without drawing any conclusions, that independently of the innumerable professional virtues demanded of him he must not be—in contrast to wily Ulysses—deaf to the song of the sirens in front of him, but blind to the arrows from their eyes.

With a good presence and a well-cut suit, or with a certain plumpness and a badly-cut suit, a conductor may still be a humbug, sometimes even without love of music. But a chorus-master cannot be a humbug! In order to succeed in shaking routine and apathy out of our choristers it is necessary, before anything else, really to love music and to think only of music, and not of oneself. There are very few who have succeeded in this, during the last twenty years.

K

While patiently knitting vocal polyphony, the choral conductor will ere long discover that the slightest loose stitch will put everything out of shape in a most lamentable fashion. Our music has its tenements, and a department of public health ought to be established without delay for the purpose of cleaning up. In France, alas, we find too often that those in leading positions surround themselves with mediocrities. How many of our greatest celebrities have made propaganda tours abroad with unworthy performers who seriously compromised French art. The *real* conductor need not fear that associating with himself real personalities will jeopardize his position. But with the incessant fear of dictators, responsibility is diluted by multiplying those responsible. And where subordinates are required, new directors are appointed instead.

We must simply ask to be obeyed and followed by those we direct, no matter how great their professional value may be. And we have to get used to not always being understood or appreciated.

The above-mentioned extract from the treatise on sacred polyphony by the choir-master of the Dijon Cathedral strikingly surveys the essential duties of the chorus conductor. It also mentions the customary professional errors. But the writer deals only with music. However, choral singing has also something to do with poetry. Choir-masters rarely worry about this at all. If they do, they do it badly and will rely only on rudimentary, arbitrary, and scientifically unfounded principles. The greatest damage to the unified singing of words is the constant error of believing that literary punctuation is the sign for taking a breath, particularly if the composer, perhaps subconsciously in the moment of creation, has transferred this punctuation into music; in other words, a wrong breath is being taken when the composer happened to put a long note on the syllable preceding a comma or semicolon.

It is a matter for the choir-master to decide whether a literary punctuation fits a melodic *caesura* or, conversely, whether the melodic line is more important than the literary rhythm. It may even happen that with a slight modification of the composer's text one achieves a more intimate approximation of his idea by restoring the continuity of the interrupted line:

It is self-evident that this first phrase of *La Damoiselle Elue* will gain when sung without taking a breath, with a tied quaver replacing the quaver's rest at the beginning of the second bar. Here Debussy interrupted the line simply for the sake of performance.

The composer is all too often in servitude to the singer who has his own peculiar illusions about the requirements of his lungs. Hence all those wrong commas right through some scores, inserted by composers themselves or by revisers. We might say that they are more a nuisance than a help. Singers always have more breath than they think, and it is enough if they know how to inhale and how to exhale economically. It is a matter for the choral conductor to demonstrate it by minutely regulating respiration, as the orchestral conductor regulates the bowing. It has also to be watched that singers, and especially choristers, do not take too long a time for breathing, to the point of distorting rhythmical exactitude.

Other errors with devastating results for vocal unity are: the phobia of elisions and tying or words. (Translator's note: naturally, this applies to the French language.) The second phrase of the same score furnishes an example of tying on the third beat of the second bar, which singers usually dodge, whereas its observance would make singing of it easier:

Indeed, the tying of the 'buzzing' 's' makes the leap of the voice easier, whereas the terrible traditional hiatus makes it difficult and hard-sounding.

Without any fear of contradicting generally accepted principles, I might express the opinion that discarding just the few above-mentioned superstitions which I chose among so many similar ones would facilitate the task for the singers themselves as well as give back to vocal music the purity of its melodic line.

Another point to notice with regard to the poetry is this: in the works of the past and in certain modern works written to old poems, the mistake is usually made of 'pronouncing' the antiquated 'oi' in some suffixes orthographically. A simple statement proves this archaeological care to be wrong: in old days, François was not pronounced like the christian name which is still used, nor Français, but Françoué. In order to get close to the ancient way of talking, we should have to apply peasant's vernacular, and this not only for a few, but for *all* words![1] It is therefore correct to stick to modern pronunciation in every case.

Goethe said: 'Does anyone ever do what he is advised to do by those who are older than he is? Everyone thinks that he knows better. That is why so many get lost for ever or at least

---

1. This is shown by rhymes in works of the past. *Le Tartuffe* gives us two examples:
   En vienne jusque là que de se méconnôitre.
   De contrarier tout, et de faire le *maître*
         Act i, Scene i
   D'autres prendraient cela d'autre façon peut-*être*
   Mais ma discretion le veut faire parôitre
         Act iii, Scene iii

run around in circles for a long time. What would be the good of our experiments and mistakes if you, the young ones, took the same path?' We must set the example, without any hope that it will be heeded, especially in our individualist country where advice is not very acceptable!

Is it possible to imagine, for instance, that the rational placing of choirs is still debated? That young conductors still persist in placing them in two groups in front of the orchestra? Debussy spoke to a friend about 'this silly custom which ought to be changed, of placing the chorus in public baths style: men on one side, women on the other. And you will see'— he added—'that great, fierce words will be used in the discussion of such a simple matter. Moreover, our age has this peculiarity, that one follows the advice of young people who have hardly learned how to walk!'

Of course, where should the resistance come from but from Metronomus, who will always be found hostile when it is a question of leaving a well-worn path? Examples from abroad do not matter to him. He will stick to this antiquated custom which was established at a time when choristers were less talented and conductors less in the habit of conducting them. For it is certainly harder work to control a massed choir from the distance. In opera, however, everything depends on the quality of the chorus-master, on the number of rehearsals, and, let us repeat it once again, on the quality of the orchestral conductor!

The same errors happen in opera where, too, the chorus are arranged in the manner of the public baths. This is easier for everyone, certainly, but sometimes the production demands something different. We have previously recalled the time when the Théâtre des Champs-Elysées and its chorus were founded. The mobility of the latter was organized in such a way that they were divided sometimes into small groups, not of the same voice-type, but of all four, so that there was always a unit of complete harmony at whatever corner of the stage it was needed. But then, of course, the chorus-master himself moved in costume among the chorus, in the manner in which they do it in some other countries outside France. The same method had been adopted at the Châtelet for the first performance of the *Martyre de St Sébastien*.

In concerts, once we have definitely agreed to renounce the nefarious human screen between the violins and the public, we should place the choir above the orchestra, right behind the last line of players. It will have been noted in chapter VIII that the tiers for the choir show only half the dimensions in depth and height. This provision was made in order to place only one row of singers on every tier, so that all of them can see the conductor.

For a normal massed choir of eighty to ninety members, four tiers will be sufficient. If there are more, the number of tiers must be proportionately increased. The placing of the voices may be done like this, beginning with the lowest:

    4th line.........Basses
    3rd „ ....Tenors
    2nd „ ....Altos
    1st „ ....Sopranos

In this manner, balance of harmony will extend all over the platform. Besides, the singers without changing their places, can be used as a double choir: for this purpose it will be enough to give each singer a number and to move odd numbers to one side and even numbers to the other.

But in case of subdivision of the four sections themselves, it will be easier to adopt the following placing:

    4th line: Tenors II   Basses II
    3rd line: Tenors I   Basses I
    2nd line: Sopranos II   Altos II
    1st line: Sopranos I   Altos I

especially when the massed choir has not many members, as is too often the case in France.

In our country of fierce individualism we never attach

enough importance to the exterior presentation of an orchestra or a massed choir. For a long time, our musicians even kicked against the rule of standing up when the conductor appeared. 'We are not lackeys', declared the fiercest ones, without considering that there is no servility in ordinary courtesy and respect.

In massed choirs, singers generally fail to rise or to sit down together. And if they consent to do so, it will often occur that, especially among the ladies, some break the rule and attract attention by bending down to adjust their skirts or to pick up a handbag.—Long live individualism! The choristers' scores should contain precise indications when to rise and when to sit down. These details must be worked out away from the orchestra, in the studio, where rehearsals ought always to take place in the formation to be adopted later for the performance.

It is wrong to neglect the exterior impression which in-fluences not only the public, but the *very performance itself*!

We do not need to go as far as at the inauguration of the Théâtre des Champs-Elysées where all the ladies had to wear white; but all of them should at least wear a white blouse without coloured decoration, and a black skirt, while the gentlemen should dress in the same manner as the orchestral players. Also, the singers should be placed according to their height, grading them so that the tallest should stand either in the centre or at the sides, whichever is more suitable. In this way, the harmonious sight of an orchestra and a choral society well arranged will favourably predispose the public. This is one of the performer's duties towards the public.

It is only fair to acknowledge here that in the Raugel choir the singers agreed in a friendly manner to adopt this visual discipline and all the other innovations which I introduced for the concert performances of certain works. First of all, 'with muted voice': simply obtained by singing with one hand in front of the mouth. Then: turning towards the centre, on the spot, until sometimes they were even standing with their backs to the audience, and then singing entirely under the direction of the choir-master who was placed at the back of the platform.[1] Then, turning back again to face the orchestral conductor. The impression of fading away and of approaching is enhanced by this simple means which resembles the principle of the organ *crescendo* and *diminuendo* effected by movable shutters. In this manner it is possible to obtain specific scenic effects in concerts. This is the result of proper work with a team of first-class assistants.

1. For in a concert also, the choir-master *must* be among the singers, as in other countries.

XII. REPETITEUR

A MAN rarely becomes répétiteur by vocation, but rather by vital necessity. Remarkable artists, having finished their studies at the Conservatoire, have resigned themselves to this profession. The reason was either simply the question of having to earn their livelihood, or some shortcoming which prevented them from becoming pianists or composers. Thus they have become répétiteurs waiting for something better which rarely turns up. It is a ladder on which one risks remaining perched until mortification sets in. At least this is the position when no team-spirit compensates for the humdrum monotony of the daily work. I should not be surprised if this position is not different abroad. Men and women, when frustrated in the same ambitions, must hang on to the same jobs. But they have quite a different conception abroad of the 'musical assistant' of whom we have already spoken.

In particular they would not be forced to work in places of the kind allotted to them in France. To begin with, French architects, when building theatres, made a point of not consulting professionals—thus, they just forgot to provide proper rehearsal rooms for singers and chorus. The latter found themselves installed in 'adapted' rooms. This was easy in the Opéra, with the considerable dimensions of the Palais Garnier. But it was not so with the Opéra-Comique, erected on much smaller premises. Thus the répétiteurs at the Salle Favart established their office in the musical library—the only convenient place —in a corner of the public foyer at the place generally reserved for the doctor on duty, or at a certain studio 37. The last, an attic, is only a lumber-room, containing the theatre accounts from its foundation day on, heaped in dusty parcels up to the ceiling! As daylight can hardly penetrate through the grimy panes, light is dispensed by an *antiquated* carbon-filament globe, in a newspaper lampshade. When I was twice director of music at this place, I asked for—at least—better lighting equipment. I never could get it from the chief electrician, who pretended that as soon as he put better globes in they were 'pinched'. Finally, there is also a certain 'suite 41' which does not get air from anywhere, and where one really rests *in pace*.

In such caverns the unfortunate répétiteurs sit at an old piano with broken notes and coach again and again a new Des Grieux, Rosine, Escamillo, and Mélisande. Yes! The very Mélisandes whom Debussy had foreseen when even in the year of the first performance he wrote to a friend: 'Now I'd like to see the *Pelléas* performances come to an end, and in a hurry! It is about time: one already begins to treat it as repertoire: the singers are improvising, the orchestra is becoming heavy—it is almost like an unreal and chimerical effort;—very shortly, *La Dame blanche* will be preferable.' And he was right. Time has indeed progressed. In the dismal haunts we have described, wrong traditions have been superimposed on *Pelléas*, as on *Carmen* and even on *La Dame blanche*. The singers themselves are the innocent prey.

'As far as the singers are concerned', a previously mentioned correspondent wrote to me, 'I have emphatically to excuse them—more, I feel sorry for them. Mostly, they are oozing good will and do what they're told. But everyone asks different things—and those poor people have to obey Maître X . . . then Maître Y . . . as well as Maître Z! That is how they're bound to become idiots—even if Toscanini himself were to conduct them!'

This is absolutely true, but it might also be said that the répétiteurs are no less to be excused, because conductors ask them for absurdities. The conductors again can be excused because they only obey the directors. The directors being no less excused because they have to surrender to politics or other factors! But no! It is necessary for the conductors to know when to say 'enough' to all those extenuating circumstances too often attached to verdicts. Far from this, the conductor, on the contrary, generally asks to be told what the 'custom' of the house is, in order to stick to it, either from ignorance or cowardice.

It can easily be imagined how piously the tradition of those principles is being kept—of those rudimentary, unscientific and arbitrary principles, of those 'major superstitions' mentioned in the preceding chapter, which have been perpetuated in the studio with the complicity of the conductors themselves.

What should a young *bâtonneur* reply to the senior coach who, of course, 'had known Debussy'! and who has prepared a very affected Mélisande, and also a Geneviève who dodges, as if it was something improper, the most natural thing:

Voici ce qu'il écrit'ha son frère Pelléas...

but who makes a special issue of all *silent* syllables:

Un jour je l'ai trouvée toute en pleurs au bord d'une fontai—NE.

And when by chance another Geneviève, previously trained in the *correct* tradition, fell into the hands of the senior coach, he mercilessly sapped her most laudable intentions. Cursed the poor woman if she failed to overdo the two slight *crescendi* in this ascending phrase:

As soon as she was thus singled out, she was heard to unburden herself: 'What the heck! This ain't right!'

Of what avail is it that the very nuances of the orchestra demand that the singer should moderate her own nuances in order to enhance the touching effect when the little boy is mentioned?

And towards the end of the season when re-engagements were negotiated, the senior coach who possessed the—misplaced—confidence of the 'boss', told that same Geneviève that she could be employed in the next year only 'in musical evenings'. . . . if any such were ever to be given, he took care to add!

The *real* conductor will tolerate the fantasy of an illustrious prima donna no more than the dubious traditions of even the best répétiteur. He is not afraid of his subordinates, that is all. The *real* conductor is not of necessity also a *great* conductor. For especially in opera one has to rate collaboration not from an ideal, but from a practical point of view. It cannot be denied that in France as elsewhere it is impossible for opera to have a sufficient number of strong or specialized personalities. It is necessary that the musical staff should include at least one 'stand-by' to whom none of the scores of 'the house' is unknown and who is able to conduct all of them—without brilliancy, but also without accidents. Only gradually can even a model opera-house breed model conductors for typical repertoire performances. Generally, one must not count too much upon obtaining a sufficient number of orchestra rehearsals for putting the repertoire performances right. Only

on exceptional occasions can a 'new production' of any
of these works really be given. As far as the other works
already 'in' the repertoire are concerned, the *bona fide* conductor must certainly know them inside out, but he should always
make it his special aim to give them, in his own approach, the
attraction of first performances. The way to achieve this is
through complete knowledge of all the wrong traditions
which have given these works the bad flavour of 'routine'.
While studying with the singers the conductor should gradually weed out all those errors for which they themselves are
not responsible, but which put into relief the guilt of the
'repertoire conductors' who from generation to generation
confined themselves merely to saying—as I have witnessed
myself—that an F sharp was 'perhaps not sufficiently sharp'
and that a quaver was 'not played at quite the correct length'!

We have to acknowledge that the younger generation
offers some hope for raising professional standards. We have
seen it while watching certain newcomers at the desk. One of
them gave the following definition of his art: 'One must
understand before one knows. One must feel before one
understands. And all the time, one must know everything.'

Yes, one must feel, understand and know everything. But
also one must try to perfect one's knowledge all the time by
following the Cartesian principle of 'taking nothing for
granted and taking anything which cannot be proved as
wrong'.

. . . I have learned not to believe too firmly in that which I have
tested only by example and custom. Thus I have gradually got rid
of many errors which are only apt to obscure our natural light and
make us less able to listen to reason.

It is necessary to possess the inner courage to think differently from the others, to refuse to admit the majority of
traditions which stem from prejudice and routine—especially
in opera! To be never afraid of finding oneself alone, and to

think that the path of those truths which no one would deny today, was slow and rough. It was even possible two centuries after the death of Descartes, whose *Discours sur la Méthode* was quoted against it, for Pasteur's theory to be rejected! Does not this fact confirm convictions which have been established by common sense? And why be surprised at perennial prejudice . . . of the obtuse confusion between rhythm and time, for example, or of the horror of emptiness? This claims that there is a 'gap' whenever the grandeur of silence should be one of the most eloquent factors of music.

My first master, perhaps among all I met the most admirable one, told us when I was hardly ten years old: 'Try to become someone real. Don't just let yourself be an anybody!' And an eminent musicologist told me when we were talking of one of these 'anybodies': 'When I was still a critic I named him *Le Bouillon Duval*, thus identifying him and his existence with the cooking at those places where you can eat without danger, but also without enjoyment'.

Especially in our period, where everyone works too fast, young conductors must beware of becoming *Bouillon Duval*.

However, those who want to be reformers must guard against two dangers:

If they want to overthrow old institutions and customs suddenly from top to bottom, they will risk creating a feeling of unrest and discontent which breeds opposition which always lies waiting at the wayside.

If they adopt the wise tactics of allowing the usual routine to establish itself in order progressively to apply reforms, they risk being themselves taken in tow by their subordinates in the quiet everyday routine, for operatic staff usually adapts itself better to underlings who stay on than to superiors who change.

It is also well known that in France, unfortunately, life is not easy for innovators. Their task is often made difficult and sometimes impossible. It is not their success which is desired, but their failure. At one of those half-hearted, half-polished revivals of *Werther*, a conductor who had once been young spent the first piano rehearsal simply in asking the singers what speeds and what nuances they had been used to at this or that passage. Afterwards in the foyer, you could hear the young chick who was to sing Sophie exclaim: 'Well, children, this will be a fine performance! *He* doesn't know one bar! He has asked *us* for our speeds!'

How much more touching was the reaction of a young Austrian musician, at first enthusiastic about our performances of Bizet's masterwork, and later disappointed by other performances: 'Well, in Austria it is always a festive occasion whenever *Carmen* is put on!'

For a conductor worthy of his name it should always be a festive occasion when he goes to the rostrum, and he should always find again the enthusiasm of his first night.

But when so many *bâtonneurs* do their work like some disagreeable duty, how could the majority of répétiteurs find it a 'festive occasion' to reopen the *Carmen* score? In long afternoons they shape Micaelas and Manons on the production line, sometimes encouraging them, sometimes discouraging them in turn, according to whether they see a potential victim for private lessons. From time to time, they risk a hint: 'Ah, my dear fellow, Mme X (their wife) would never allow you to do it like this! By the way, your voice is placed too far back, not enough in the mask . . . your voice is badly placed . . . it would not be difficult to cure you. . .!'

And when you consider that the conductors, the producers, and so many others also sometimes have wives who want a similar share in their husbands' jobs, you may imagine what the poor singer will think—and especially the poor singer who *is* poor!

Why is it that singers always sing loudly? Simply because, banging on their tumble-down pianos, the répétiteurs often omit getting them used to nuances which they themselves do not observe. And the conductor does not care, either, because at the full stage rehearsal he will mark the time by tapping with his baton against the edge of his stand. In some opera houses, you may even behold a stand in which the wood has worn away at a certain place at which the conductor always hammers.

However, the position of the répétiteur can be fine and honoured. How proud was I when in my youth I was allowed for the first time to do a 'stage rehearsal'! For if it can be interesting to prepare the singers strictly musically for their rôles, it is not less interesting to go on stage with them and to collaborate from the wings. This is another of the activities of the 'musical assistant' which consists of co-ordinating with the orchestra everything which takes place off-stage, especially when the conductor himself is interested in this department of operatic performing. And when, discarding an antiquated traditionalism which I have mentioned elsewhere (author's *Diabolus in Musica*, chapter 18), he knows how to let his assistants have the upper hand, according to the Berlioz principle 'that an operatic conductor must know how to act as accompanist for everything that happens off-stage in opera'.

Thus, fruitful team-work can be accomplished, as we have said at the end of the preceding chapter and also previously, when comparing a conductor's assistants with a surgeon's assistants.

Among the conductor's assistants, only those are justified in their existence who take a passionate interest in the Coronation Scene bells of *Boris Godounov*—and in stopping them neatly— who find the bell for the matins in Pimen's cell moving and the death-bell for the Czar agonizing, and who care for the trumpet announcing the arrival of the false Dimitri in the last scene, and for the distant revolution-bell during the last lines of the idiot; who are anguished at the idea that the gun in *L'Etoile* won't go off at their command. What are they doing in *Freischütz*? They unfetter the elements, they count the

'echo' of the bullets cast under Samiel's spell, they thrash the
imaginary horses of the black hunt, and sound the bell indicating the first hour of morning in the deep silence at the end of
the *Wolf's Glen* scene. And then they must feel like telling you
that with a few more performances like this, they will probably die in the flower of their youth!

Those young men have understood. Like the surgeon's
assistants, they know how to calm the patient's fears of the
forthcoming operation; they know how to reassure the poor
singers just about to 'offend the boss'. Even confidences are
exchanged in their studios, and stories told. We learn from a
worthy baritone who has just been pulled up for singing too
loudly that one of his tenor friends tortured himself to find an
alteration of words which would furnish him with the dental
consonant necessary for his 'powerful' high C at the end of
Faust's already quoted Cavatine, and that the fellow had
ultimately found his way out like this:

Cavatine de Faust

As a compensation, we find that a 'damoiselle élue', anguished by a 'silent "e"', tells us that the syllable will succeed
with ease, helped by the orchestral *forte*, if one only sticks to
the 'ah' sound of the preceding syllable and actually suppresses
the 'e' sound of the last syllable, and then pronounces the con-
sonants not on the tone to which they belong, but after it, like
this:

La Damoiselle Élue

L

And one makes use of the opportunity by telling the tenor who happens to be present that other 'silent "e" vowels' are no less harmful. For instance those which make the Aubade of the *Roi d'Ys*—which, of course, he sings so very well!—sound heavy! One will convince him that by simply suppressing them he will still add to the charm of this exquisite piece in which, nevertheless, he ought to be careful not to spoil the flavour of the triplets by hurrying them:

Le Roi d'Ys
(Aubade)

Vai_ne_ment   ma bien-ai _ mé _ ♩   On   croit me dé _

_ ses_pé_rer   Près de la por _ _ _ _ te fer _ mé _ ♩

Thus, the willing singers can be shown how to overcome some vocal difficulty or another by intelligent handling instead of by some stunt of the larynx.

We should add perhaps that the suppression of 'silent "e" vowels' has its contradictions. This is the case when uniform pronunciation of the syllables is based on the line of rhythm or melody, as in the first phrase of the female narrator in *La Damoiselle Elue*:

La Damoiselle Elue

Sa ro-be flot-tan-te n'é- taitpointor-née de fleursbro-

dé - es   Mais d'u-ne ro-se blan-che,   pré-sent de Ma-

ri - e   Pour le   di - vin   ser-vi - ce

Exceptions from established laws of pronunciation can only be decided by taste.

When musical assistants consider their profession in this light, the need for them becomes self-explanatory. And even when one cannot work with a 'boss' of one's choice, it is always possible to watch others with amusement, like the 'subtle friend' who wrote me:

> We are in the middle of rehearsing. The orchestral parts of the work are full of mistakes. The composer has himself added them to the orchestration which someone else has made for him. In addition, there are the usual mistakes in the orchestral parts, and in addition those of the copyist, plus those which the composer has made when he wanted to correct the copyist. (Especially in the transposing instruments.) After which, the orchestra makes, in addition, its own usual mistakes, and in the course of rehearsing, conductor and composer show the orchestra how to make some more; no one knows any more where he stands. On stage are my poor lost chicks, the completely idiotic composer, juggling with B naturals and B flats in crazy sarabands! At first I've tried to help them, but they prefer making mistakes. Well, I quickly capitulated, thinking that, perhaps, it will be more fun this way. And now for the first performance!

The *bâtonneurs* are never aware that not only the orchestral players judge them. . . .

Oh, those transposing instruments! I remember a certain 'modern' score of the 'Ballets Russes' which I had to conduct and in which a passage seemed to me 'involuntarily' wrong. I compared it with the piano score. And then I noticed that the composer had marked a wrong clarinet transposition. The composer and all the conductors who had been conducting the work for years on end must have 'preferred' the mistake! I found it equally good fun not to make any correction—perhaps there will be one day another 'subtle friend' after me who will think that I had not noticed anything, either!

XIII. VOCE, VOCE, E POI VOCE

A PAINTING or a book may be considered as finished when the painter or the writer has put away his brush or his pen. The work of the musician, once written and printed, can never—or almost never—be helped or defended by its author; it depends on the interpreters who, in order to perform it, often resort to dubious and distorting 'compromises'.

In music it is necessary to rebuild a work from its very foundations whenever a performance takes place. With the performances, this often leads to a shapeless state of affairs which is more depressing than anything else for a conductor. For it is infinitely hard to be pitiless with worn-out, tired people when making them perform for the thousandth time the C Minor Symphony or the *Carmen* quintet. You may certainly comfort yourself with this ideal: that there is no greater satisfaction than to do your work well, and honestly to fulfil your vocation. But this is where the misunderstanding begins, for everyone among the performers is generally convinced that he is doing the same.

There is nothing better—despite disillusions which assail you, and despite the feeling of getting tired of it all which is in store for you—than to attend those places where noble precision work is the law. Let us go to the circus or to the music-hall which Colette has immortalized, and let us not smile at the way the ring events are announced:

EXCEPTIONAL ATTRACTION!

LES WALTON'S
the latest spectacle
of jaw and tight-rope.

Every night, the Latest Spectacle will be performed conscientiously and with the same easy precision. In this manner
Barbette, Rastelli or Colleano do their routine wherever they
may be, despite the pains and joys of their unconventional
existence. True, the slightest carelessness can spell death to the
acrobat, and Rastelli's excessive nervous tension hastened his
end. Nevertheless it is likely that they themselves think much
less of danger than of the disgrace they would risk if they were
to 'spoil' their act.

For the man who is at the helm of a musical interpretation,
nothing can be more desirable than the conscientious precision
of those who participate. However, nothing is more in
abeyance in most cases, and especially in France. It is already
difficult to keep an orchestra attentive enough to play 'what is
written'. The difficulty increases when there are choirs, and
becomes still more uncomfortable when solo singers are concerned in addition.

We will now talk of singers.

Chaliapine has been credited with this declaration: 'When
I come on stage, I think only of my worst enemy: the conductor!' This simply proves that one of the greatest artists and
greatest singers, the unforgettable Boris, was the prey of some
megalomania quite unworthy of his past. In order to keep
intact the memory of his glory, conductors worthy of their
name should henceforth have refused this unequal and futile
duel with an old man.

Everything should be done to avoid that state of affairs when
the orchestra pit becomes for the singer a trench which separates
him from the 'enemy'. It is a problem which just the greatest
among the singers and the greatest among the conductors
should be able to solve. But we have to confess that the matter
has become singularly difficult in our age of speed and improvisation. A singer and a conductor have scarcely sized each
other up across the trench before they part again for months,
for years, without having had time for talking, and often

taking badly found opinions of each other away with them, established by some misunderstanding! All of them should know and think for a moment about the word of Sophocles —who, after all, was one of the greatest figures of the theatre: 'Treat your friend as if one day he may be your enemy, and treat your enemy as if one day he may be your friend'.

Before anything else, conductors should talk frankly and in a friendly manner with the singers. But not with the cowardice of certain répétiteurs or certain conductors, on the prowl for private pupils.

The unfortunate singers fall only too often into the trap of the private-lesson racket which consists in blaming them for a grave mistake when what they have done was a slight oversight. This is how the illusory 'treatment' by private lessons can be prolonged. And the hope for an engagement or a certain rôle will be dangled before them.

The art of singing is not blossoming at present. No one, indeed, fails to acknowledge the inferior standard of the French opera-houses, in comparison with former times. The sudden arrival of some strong personalities would not change the situation: at most it might bring about a change in some superficial minds.

The appearance of these 'stars' is not subject to any law. They will just be there, spontaneously, at their proper hour, in groups or isolated, and even at a period when artistic standards are low. We have to consider the whole question from a broader point of view and take as issue the quality of a whole operatic ensemble in order to gauge the gravity of the crisis, its origin, and the appropriate remedies.

Chaliapine would probably have attributed the manner of characterization with which the last two paragraphs dealt, to the hostility of some 'worst enemy'. However, I cunningly omitted quotation-marks, and the description did not emanate from some bad-tempered conductor. All singers ought to be able to recognize the source: for they are the beginning lines of one of the most admirable books which an illustrious predecessor has left them. I have alluded (author's *Diabolus in Musica*, chapter 16) previously to Faure's *La Voix et le Chant*. It remains surprising that most singers still ignore this work, which should be a bible for all. And it is strange how every reference in it is still valid when one tries to talk today, as objectively as possible, of the decadence of singing in France.

At the time, Faure attributed this decadence to the following factors: (1) The proper practising of religious music had almost gone out of existence owing to the suppression of choirschools which up to that time had actually *formed* generations of singers from childhood on. (2) The type of modern musical compositions which do not compel singing students any longer to perfect themselves in vocal gymnastics. Vocal virtuosity did not occur in these works and therefore appeared superfluous. (3) The vagueness and uncertainty of singing methods at the Conservatoire. He mentions in addition the trend which singers have of shaping themselves according to the public's demands, and of following all the variations of public taste in order to achieve popularity. This latter point was one of the reasons for the warning which he issued concerning all voices. This warning, among many other things which still apply today, deserves elucidation.

As to the classification of voices, Faure says first—underlining it—that it must be made rather according to the timbre than according to range. He distinguished between dramatic tenor, lyric tenor, first comic opera tenor, high baritone (Verdi rôles), basso cantante (bass-baritone), and basso profondo. Female voices: high soprano, dramatic soprano, mezzo-soprano, and contralto.

We have mentioned already the errors of most directors and conductors or of répétiteurs with regard to voices. This does not refer to technique which concerns only the singers, but to the simple point of the character or timbre, and its possibilities.

To let the same tenor sing Don José and Almaviva, and the same soprano Manon and Tosca, certainly looks on the surface like economy, and like added advantages for singers. However, it is neither. The director has engaged too many singers—and especially female ones!—and too cheaply, often also in order to meet too many obligations of a not quite strictly musical kind. . . . He could spend less money, pay higher fees, and give better performances. The benefit reaped by the tenor and the soprano is illusory because their voices will last for a shorter time and not sound so well, that is all!

The actual crisis in singing concerns the high voices and particularly tenors. So much so that we might ask ourselves whether the latter sort of voice is not becoming altogether extinct. Formerly, every opera-house had at least one of the various types mentioned by Faure. Actually on the day he leaves the Conservatoire, the present-day young tenor will be bought up by directors and impresarios who compete with each other in making him useless, after some ten years of overworking him. It is the same with high sopranos.

The dearth of dramatic tenors and lyric tenors induces the light tenors to sing rôles beyond their vocal resources. They 'force' their voices until they get a 'wobble' which will not leave them again. In order to 'sing' like a dramatic tenor they have abandoned the head voice, the charming *falsetto* which allowed them to sing some high notes with a logic dictated by their voices. When they want to apply *falsetto* again, they won't be able to do it any more.

Besides, there exists a silly prejudice against *falsetto*, a consequence of the ignorance of singers as well as of the public. It is generally taken for granted that *falsetto* means that a singer uses a trick, facilitates his task and takes a short cut. Nothing could be more untrue. Faure himself confirmed it. The man who first created Mephisto was probably thinking of certain Faust interpreters who brought 'their' Cavatine in the Garden Scene to a wrong conclusion. Having saluted for the last time *la demeure chaste et pure*, they made three steps towards the footlights, stretched out their fist and sent to the public their most powerful

Ou se devine la pré . . .

but uncertain of their chest 'C', they whispered suddenly in *falsetto*, without transition, the one syllable 'sen . . .', only to resume again immediately their most powerful 'chest-voice' with the full force of their lungs, of course: '. . . *ce* (which they pronounce 'ça') *d'une âme innocente et divine*'.

This is, of course, something very different from what one calls 'the art of singing' and resembles more that of the ventriloquist who makes the voice of the 'ickle piggy' reply to the 'big bad oolf.'

It is simply a matter of knowing how to use this register of the voice, by working for a 'transition between chest and *falsetto* register, known to be one of the most effective means for making the flexibility of the voice complete', wrote Faure. And he added: 'This register, skilfully applied, will render most valuable services to all tenors as well as to light baritones. Therefore I recommend them to perfect and to use it.' Perhaps one should not make the same remark concerning the use of special 'whitening' of the voice which is so often misused. When applying or when discarding it, greatest caution is necessary. On the other hand, the remarks do apply to the female chest-voice.

For conductors who have often to conduct singers it will be a great help if they are able to make remarks and recommendations which are supported by and in complete accord with a master such as Faure. We have dealt with *falsetto* and are presently going to deal with *legato* and articulation. All the time the same argument of the great singer confirms the opinion of the musician: work! you must work!

If one of the acrobats we have mentioned did not train every day just as much as before the first performance, he would risk killing or crippling himself for the rest of his life. The career of singing would be tragically depleted if a mistake of the 'Latest Spectacle of the jaw' were to be as deadly to the false steps of Euterpe as it is to the false notes of Icarus.

The famous first Mephisto devotes the last part of his *Traité pratique* to 'Remarks and advice for young singers'. It is a special pleasure to see him disapprove of that deplorable habit of 'rehearsing down in your shoes' which is the (French) professional jargon for not using one's full voice at rehearsals or singing high passages an octave lower. 'This procedure may expose the singer to unpleasant surprises when before the public, and leads almost always to hoarseness and often even to complete misfiring of a top note. A singer must rehearse in the same way in which he is going to perform.'

Faure advised avoiding sports, long walks, or drives before singing, because jolting and vibration is always damaging to the voice. What would he have thought of the motor-car which enabled a singer to add still more to his purse?

Then Faure finishes thus:

> Many people find it really difficult to sing in the morning. There is only one way of triumphing over these indispositions and of getting rid of the passing hoarseness which generally follows sleep and disappears with certain artists only after the first meal: this is to do singing exercises every day while getting up. This I call 'La Toilette de la Voix'. I cannot recommend too strongly these morning exercises the advantages of which I personally was always able to feel.

And this 'toilette of the voice' consists of no less than twenty-one exercises which by themselves occupy the last twenty-five pages of the volume and which must be multiplied by twelve, because each of them ought to be repeated from each chromatic semitone!

Could a young painter who had received the inspiration of

real work from the Flemish school, suddenly give up hasty
working and paint as slowly as a van Eyck or a Breughel? He
would never be able to earn a living...! Similarly, young
singers, alas, can no longer follow the wise advice of vocal
hygiene as given by the great Faure.

Once it was possible to force artists to sing only at the opera-
houses to which they belonged. Today, management cannot
prevent them accepting additional fees elsewhere and even
have to advise them to do so in order to increase their insufficient income. Instead of paying the singers more for fewer
performances, they are forced to sing too much, risking their
singing badly. And this is the chief reason for the crisis of
French singing. The fact is that a bodily organ like the larynx
deteriorates when not made flexible by regular discipline. The
singers neglecting virtuoso exercises are obliged (under the
pretext of having to make the required impression upon the
audience) to take refuge in tricks—which do not deceive
anyone.

Not only is it almost impossible for them ever to interpret
a *bel canto* work, but the execution of its ornaments and em-
broideries has become an almost insurmountable difficulty for
most of them. These little notes, these appoggiaturas, grup-
petti, and turns which were once called *agréments*, might
today only too often be called *disagreements*! Concerning the
trill described by Duprez as 'a sound trembling in an artistic
manner', it is too often replaced simply by a 'trembling tone',
the forerunner of the wobble, the consequence of suppression
or insufficiency of exercises for 'placing' the voice.

Singers and conductors never think enough of the state in
which passages with several notes on the same vowel *reach* the
public. The following example can give them an idea: the
large notes are naturally accentuated by the articulation of the
syllables. The small notes will mostly be inaudible.

Vo_ tre_ tour-te ... rel . le_ vous_ e . chap . . pe.ra

Romeo et Juliette (Gounod) Chanson du page

In order to counteract this frequent error, it is enough to study a passage like this with accents on the unaccentuated notes

Vo.o_ tree_ tour ou_ le e_

as pianists do in exercises for the weak (fourth and fifth) fingers, and as we have recommended for the orchestra in chapter VI.

The same error can also be found in choral music and remedied in the same fashion. We said above that neither singer nor conductor thinks sufficiently of the state in which what is being sung 'comes over' to the public. On the other hand, the public does not sufficiently often show its displeasure when it could do so.

Returning for a moment to the 'silent "e" ' of the preceding chapter, let us call the public as witness:

> French music, at least vocal music, has so far failed to please any other nation. It could not possibly please other people because its prosody is different from all others. We always stress the last French syllable, whereas all the other nations accentuate the second last or third last, like the Italians. Our language is the only one with words ending in silent 'e', and these 'e', not pronounced in ordinary talking, are pronounced in musical declamation, and this in a uniform manner, 'gloi-reu', 'victoi-reu' 'barbari-eu', 'fu-rieu' . . . this is what makes our arias and our recitatives unbearable for anyone not used to it.

That is how Voltaire expressed it, long ago, in his *Artistes célèbres*.

As the State can grant our opera-houses only insufficient subsidies, we have to resign ourselves to being unable to rival the great opera-houses abroad, and to have to call on their great singers or even on their whole ensembles whenever we want to give really homogeneous interpretations of the works of Wagner, Mozart, or Verdi. All the same we ought to try to check the horrible state of mediocrity from which France is suffering at the present time. The first thing is to stop over-working the good singers we still have—because there still are some. Would not this safeguard the proper presentation of our national works? And the public might contribute by abandoning its apathy and by refusing to tolerate a situation in which second-rate artists are presented to it as great singers.

Furthermore, it is necessary completely to reorganize the teaching of singing and operatic art in France. And lastly it is necessary to put our singers themselves on guard against those of their imperfections which they can and must correct without delay.

Alas, it is clear that they have not got the time to work as steadily as their predecessors. But must they cut down work quite as much as they do? They recall a certain eminent conductor, overburdened with different jobs, who naïvely declared he always felt happy when he had a score 'under his arm'. But conductors, like singers or instrumentalists, should not have to worry any more about scores or any other personal work to be done, once they are assembled to work together with the others. But this 'ideal' state of affairs has become very rare, and most of the time the artists give a very clear impression of acting every man for himself. Not being in a fit state to think of anything but the letter, they must of necessity neglect the spirit. Therefore it happens that performances usually take on the appearance of a 'one-price' store. In French theatrical jargon one speaks of actors as playing *au cann*, or *à la broch*, according to whether they respect the words (*brochure*) or whether they are satisfied with only giving a sketch (*canevas*) of their role. The professional obligation of singing from memory forces overworked singers to sing *au cann*, cramming the music into their heads in a hasty 'almost right' fashion, without taking the time to deepen their understanding of the literary contents. An incomprehensible flood oozes from the stage as a result, without the slightest relation to the 'sustained *legato* singing', the rules for which Faure gives with so much clarity:

> This is what orchestral musicians call 'playing without the bow leaving the strings'. For singing *legato*, it is necessary closely to unite the sounds. Although the words may tend to disunite them, there must be no interruption of the continuity. In order to sustain the singing line at the same time, it is also necessary to handle the transitions from *forte* to *mezzoforte* and between all other dynamic gradations so that these transitions become imperceptible, which requires a great amount of will-power. But it assures for the voice perfect homogeneity, the homogeneity on which depends the musical phrase.
>
> One must consider sustained *legato* singing as one of the most powerful means of expression. In the apparently so simple application of this procedure lies one of the deepest and most precious secrets of the art of singing. But one must beware of confusing this means with the miserable counterfeit used by certain singers which consists of a continuous ooah-ooah, resembling the wheeze of an accordion.

There is also a manner of hesitantly spluttering phrases which ought to be sung properly which reminds us of Morse, the more so as it is often impossible for the listener to understand the slightest word. During an opera, one catches a passing single word every now and then, like a piece of cake from an overcrowded buffet. With this we have arrived at the super-sensitive issue of *articulation*.[1] Unfortunately, we may

1. Translator's note: 'The applying (as in the original French) of the three words "articulation", "pronunciation" and "diction" is intentional in order to convey the three different shades of meaning. The words are neither loosely applied nor interchangeable.'

have to blame far too many of our French singers in this respect. And this will be in the nature of a warning to put them on guard against a substantial danger which may have very serious results. Most of our singers lack the ability to articulate. This is becoming more and more unbearable now that so many performances are broadcast and therefore are indirect and calculated for an invisible, innumerable and critical audience.

On this point, too, we shall refer to a great singer whose long and glorious career can still be remembered by the young generation, a great operatic artist one of whose peculiarities was that he never allowed one single word he sang to get lost.

In a book on Lucien Fugère we learn how the great singer came to pay special attention to his articulation:

> It was Gounod who at the beginning of my career told me of one of the primary necessities of the art of singing: 'My dear friend, I happen to know the music of my opera much better than you', he told me one day. 'It is the words which I am keen to hear.' I realized what he meant. Henceforth, I gave all my attention to articulation. You must articulate as if there was nothing to it, and so that the public thinks there is nothing to it. When articulating one always gives enough voice. . . .

Then he quotes the great actor Coquelin, who maintained that

> *Articulation* is at the same time the basis and the highest point of art. You have to learn it at the outset, as children have to learn how to be polite, because articulation is the courtesy of actors, as punctuality is the courtesy of kings. And then, you have to exercise the same courtesy all throughout your life. It is on purpose that I define it as courtesy: for indeed, you are addressing the public and thus you have to be understood, viz., you have to articulate clearly.
> If I have preserved my voice, Fugère went on, 'it is because I understood early that the *voice* is not the aim of singing, but a means for singing, put at the service of thought. Therefore I have disciplined my voice and made it obey all demands of expression. So I have always aimed at linking articulation and music. When I

work at a rôle, I do not occupy myself with the voice but with the diction. The voice comes quite by itself. I sing my rôle with the same expression as I would if I were to declaim it. In one word: I sing as I speak.

Fugère, we are also told, must have embarrassed more than one music-lover when he humorously declared:

Obviously, it is impossible to sing without voice, but voice is not enough for operatic expression. Often voice is even prejudicial to it. With a richly resonant voice it happens—if the singer does not know (or not sufficiently) how to articulate—that 'tone eats word', that 'vowel eats consonant', and that 'the voice makes holes in the articulation'. The singer then 'makes so much noise that one doesn't hear him' and that one doesn't understand him. The most beautiful piece will thus be transformed into a singing exercise, and does not express anything and loses all its charm.

The singer who is only interested in his voice takes the servant for the master: he forgets the aim of singing which is to express and therefore, to articulate. The voice, that's all very well—but the public has come to hear the piece. The public knows a singer's voice after ten minutes. What interests the public is the action of the piece, the expression, and the actor's acting. The public wishes to see him 'live' his rôle, not to stand like a stick in the middle of the stage.

There is really only one rational method of learning singing, viz., to practise phonetic difficulties (i.e. articulation which contains all of them) by combining these difficulties with those of the music and the voice (intonation, accents of pitch and of intensity, sustaining of sounds, etc...), *but always as a function of the emotional quality*, that is, with a colour of tone which renders the voice significant. And to learn how to change this vocal quality according to the individual sentiments to be expressed.

Singers too often neglect the end by allowing the means to predominate. In order to move the listener, they must forget voice and rolling RRR and think only of the words... after having learned their notes properly.

As Faure left singers his invaluable *Traité pratique*—almost unknown to them—Fugère wrote for them his new practical method *Chant Français par l'Articulation*. On the first pages he reveals that lack of articulation is one of the reasons for bad pronunciation. Singers generally make their exercises on isolated vowels and especially on 'ah', 'which has nothing to do with pronunciation, as this very vowel "a" hardly ever occurs by itself but mostly in the middle of a syllable or a word'. And then, Fugère shows how to unite constant articulation exercises with exercises for the placing of the voice, simply by adopting not vowels but whole syllables, the living element of the words the very laws of which must be adopted for singing.

Of course, Fugère agrees with Faure on sustained *legato*. He advises using tying and elision, those phobias of singers who are always trying to hide them as if they were unseemly. Let us mention here the erroneous idea of punctuation in singing, viz., to think that the most unimportant comma automatically means a breath. The composer generally indicates his ideas of when a breath ought to be taken, by musical punctuation, that is, by the way he uses note-values in the rhythm.

I am glad that Fugère mentions the tying of syllables which is one of the secrets of good articulation. 'In singing, the *vowel* of a syllable should be attacked precisely on the note meant for this syllable.' He then shows a slightly complicated method of how to achieve it, but one might simplify it by saying that for clear articulation it is sufficient to pronounce the first consonant of a syllable as if belonging to the end of the preceding syllable.

We could go on quoting ad infinitum some line or the other from these two remarkable books which would enable all singers, through the advice of their illustrious predecessors, to master for themselves those phonetic difficulties which they believe to be vocal ones. Unfortunately, singers in general pay too much attention to what is written *about* them and not enough to what is written *for* them. Then, when an accident occurs, they 'go to the doctor', generally the more dangerous the more specialized he is! They may also go to a 'quack'. This

M

is what one may call certain enterprising people who succeed in a short time in taking from the poor singers all their assurance and all that was *natural* in their singing. For the French singer too often is unable to acknowledge a purely vocal method which fits the words and the style of his country. So-called 'specialized' singing masters advocate the German school of singing in opposition to the *bel canto* method, in the same manner in which the Italian and the Flemish school of painting excluded one another. Snobbery helping on the wrong side, we have seen the sad changes in French singers who gradually lost all their faculty for ease and spontaneity and ultimately gave a hoarse and guttural flavour to the language of Molière and the music of Rameau who, after all, were nearer to Alessandro Scarlatti and Dante than to Goethe and Wagner.

Could one imagine one of our violinists rejecting the fruits of all his past studies in favour of a sudden adoption of German technique? It is true that our composers themselves have not yet completely recovered from Wagnerism, and that the Russians try to escape from Slavonic influence! If it is true that art knows no frontiers, it is also true that great nations have an art of their own. It would be the apex of wisdom to learn how to profit from all achievements abroad and how to stay at home, at the same time. Thus, Debussy and Moussorgsky, universally human, have remained French and Russian.

Before concluding this chapter, let us quote Faure twice more:

> I do not know to which maestro the peculiar sophism is attributed that for singing three things are necessary: *Voce, voce, e poi voce.* He forgot style, taste, and feeling which are as essential to singers as to composers or instrumentalists.
>
> Asked many a time to sing Verdi's baritone rôles, I believed I must resist the temptation of increasing my repertoire by many magnificent rôles which I should have been very happy to interpret; but they are written in a *tessitura* which my vocal resources forbade me to attempt.

Conductors ought to know these things in order to tell the singers. Thus, the latter could be cautioned against errors such as those described in the two preceding chapters; notably that referring to the pronunciation of old French.

In order to know our craft well, we have to know more than our craft. And in order to do our craft well, we must not try to do more than our resources permit.

It is only in order to fulfil what I considered my duty that I have given in to the temptation of making all these 'deviations'. President Barthou, who loved music as passionately as professional integrity, sanctioned them once and commented as follows, with a little grain from his own great store of wisdom: 'I greatly fear that few people will follow you! But never mind! One must do one's duty even if it is useless!'

XIV. PRODUCER

Particularly in France, musicians have to be always prepared for disagreements—not only with the singers, but also with directors and producers. The latter are often inclined to go beyond their domain and to interfere with the musician's task, particularly when long experience has given them some rudimentary knowledge of our art. 'Nothing is as much of a nuisance as people who know a *little* about music', once said Vincent d'Indy.

Anywhere else but in France the authority of the producer is subordinated to the conductor. In Italy, indeed, the latter decides personally on the production.

It would be undesirable to make this power of the Transalpine conductors a general custom. Although it may exist in some cases, the gift of such an amount of versatility is too rare to be set up as a principle. The best conductor may only be a mediocre scenic animator. His preoccupation with subjecting the stage to his baton may act as a curb on his producing. It is preferable for the production to be in the hands of a producer. He must be free from responsibility for anything musical. And he must always be ready to give in to music whenever the conductor demands. This is the usage in Russia, in Germany—in fact, anywhere else except in France.

Whether the producer is a musician or not is of little importance. The essential factor is that he must come 'from the theatre', as the conductor must come 'from the orchestra'. This was the case with Albert Carré, who always respected the elementary rights of music, even though he pretended not to understand anything about it. Therefore he was a great director and a great producer. Generally speaking, production is confused with stage-management—a fact which so often gives mediocre subalterns a chance to show off.

The conductor therefore has a noble duty to fulfil but seldom does so, through cowardice or indifference. Often even worthwhile conductors have surrendered. It is only too easy to adopt a disdainful silence in the face of mere 'supervisors', too often unable to direct an operatic scene. By kow-towing to them, their presumption will be encouraged, and jokes aimed at them *behind their backs*, witty as they may be, do not defend music against them. And music, one day, will take its own vengeance for this sort of attitude.

With simple courage and integrity a conductor can brave an incompetent pocket-dictator. He can also demand and get everything from the personnel. But it is often because of a feeling of their own insecurity that a number of conductors prefer to compromise. Not daring to show that he has character in case he might commit a blunder, and to resort to the eternal opportunist's 'what's the use' when faced by an enormous task, is the greatest danger for the young conductor. The more so if around him he can only see examples of mediocrity.

The producer has to do his work without worrying beforehand about the music. The servile assimilation of music and gesture, as advised by certain primers, is as stupid as that imitation-mania of some films: the running of horses or of men must 'thunder'; a letter crushed in one's hand or torn up must be accompanied by the appropriate noise; a glass must be filled with a gurgle.

If co-ordination becomes more important than the action, it will rob the latter of all realism. This happens in opera when *Fidelio* prisoners are made to march in step.

Further examples of puerile gestures as comment on words: A thumb pointing over his shoulder when the suitor sings in *Pénélope*, 'I saw two cawing ravens pass on my left'. 'Make your gestures before you say "on my left" so that everyone can understand!' demands the professor to the general amusement of his personnel. The same in *Boris* when Gregory replies to the policeman, in the inn scene: 'I am from the next village and accompany these two pilgrims'.

But elsewhere, the same producer, so concerned with realism, will not notice that off-stage music is generally placed too close because he forgets that painted canvas walls behind which it plays are not making it sound distant. The same applies to off-stage choirs. But then, we should not lose sight of the fact that he actually should not confine himself to too unconditional realism. Because according to whether this distant music is supposed to be hardly noticeable or whether its sound is supposed to be actually on top of the orchestral sound, its real dynamics will have to be modified in order always to be heard and in order to *seem* always uniform, from the point of view of the listener.

At the time when M. Jacques Rouché was in charge of the destiny of our national opera-house, I was one day in his office. In his huge room at the Opéra the antique furniture was in harmony with the place and gave it an intimate atmosphere which tempered the solemnity.

In the centre, on a large oblong table, you could see numerous models of operatic scenery and also a scale-model of the old theatre at Orange where the director had just put on some operatic performances. Alluding to them, I asked M. Rouché his impressions and he replied: 'It is now perfectly clear to me that the décor was not of the slightest importance'.

This declaration was surprising, coming from a man who had devoted so many years to the theatre and whose particular attention was always focussed on the décor. I have often pondered over these words of his which may be extended to everything which contributes to the scenic presentation of musical works. And one of M. Jacques Rouché's successors supplemented him in a very clear manner by declaring that in opera the law should always be: 'Music first'.

But it is not enough just to say so in order to satisfy the

musician. It would be necessary to make him realize that something has drastically changed in French opera where for such a long time the law had been 'stage first' and even 'scenery first'. This was very noticeable during a noisy revival of *Pelléas* where Maeterlinck and Debussy were not as important as a certain modernist of the palette whose ideal it was to suppress any trace of vegetation in the forests as well as in the gardens of the old king of Allemonde!

We could say a lot on the subject of the scene-painter's instrusion into the world of opera. In this respect we are always referred to the example of the Russians. But is not this rather a special proof that Léon Bakst, Nicolas Roerich, Alexander Benoît and Golovine had found their *real* avocation in theatre décor? The truth is, then, that the art of *certain* painters, but not of all of them, is suitable for theatre decoration.

But let us return to the producer and to his outlook in relation to music. Bernard Zimmer used to tell the story of how he was watching an ultra-modern production of *Phèdre* put on by a Russian producer. He had expressed his surprise to the latter at his bold attitude towards Racine's tragedy. Without hesitation, the Muscovite retorted: 'But Racine only wrote the words!' How many producers—and even conductors and singers—act as if they think the composers have 'only written the notes'!

The conductor should always insist on respect for the composer's idea which he represents. He should prevent the scenic realization from departing from or even damaging a good musical execution. This is the custom at Vienna or at La Scala, where everything is dictated by the requirements of the music. The strangest result is that the scenery often gains through it. In France, where people obstinately refuse to follow the example of other countries, things are being complicated instead of simplified. Every attempt at reform dashes its head against a wall of outworn tradition. Let us take as an example the coronation scene of *Boris*, where the choruses represent the crowd of the people acclaiming the Czar as he crosses the stage from the parvis of one cathedral to the opposite cathedral. More than half the choristers turn their backs on the conductor, sometimes turning their heads in order to throw a glance at the baton, for *of course* there is no chorus-master in costume present among his sheep to help them with his voice or with a glance.[1] But it would be quite easy to replace the first ranks of choristers who turn their back on the conductor by extras, and to mass *all* the choristers on the other side of the path to be taken by Boris. In this way they could face the conductor, and their voices would go directly to the audience.

At the beginning of *Ariane et Barbe Bleue* the chorus of excited peasants off-stage must be heard very distinctly, and the composer has stipulated that certain isolated voices should be placed as near the orchestra as possible. These are the voices which throw the necessary light on the action. But Dukas's strong orchestration prevents them from penetrating to the audience. Someone then came to the brilliant idea of actually moving this 'off-stage' business on to the stage: When the curtain rises, and before the scenery of the first act is seen, gesticulating peasants appear on stage behind a gauze curtain. They act. They burst out with their isolated replies which ought to have been off-stage, thus robbing the drama of all its mystery. Here it would have been right to reverse the procedure and to solve the problem by placing the isolated voices at the back of the orchestra pit. Thus scenic balance and balance of sound would have been restored.

It is strange that in other works experiments aiming at simplification had clearly been successful. They should then have been more generally used, especially in *La Damnation de Faust* for the Easter Chorus and Le Menuet des Follets, and in the last scene of *Roi d'Ys*. But here the producer, thinking

1. Some reform on these lines has meanwhile been attended to.

purely of the stage, had really served music in spite of himself. In opera there exists a sort of mystical desire for complication. Thus the electrical time-beater is still being used too much, whereas it ought to be applied only in exceptional cases. For it has many shortcomings described elsewhere (author's *Diabolus in Musica*, chapter 18).

This mystical desire for complication induces a producer to 'animate' an aria or a duet—whatever the costs in the way of logic and commonsense.

Commonsense is not a tool of evolution—wrote Count Noüy—
it is purely a personal and practical issue, of no value for human progress. A certain amount of commonsense is as necessary as salt in food, but its absence has better results than its excess. (*L'Avenir de l'Esprit*.)

As long as opera exists, we shall have to cope with its conventions and its nonsense, the principal one being that what would otherwise be spoken is being *sung*, and that the characters move always in rooms with one side missing.

When in 1925 I put on *Tristan* at the Opéra-Comique, King Mark was sung by Felix Vieuille, the unforgettable first Arkel, who was worried because he had to stand still all through his famous 'tale' in the second act. I advised him to forget his costume and the scenery at this moment of the opera and to behave as if he was simply singing the famous passage at a concert. Then he found, with his customary ease, the right interpretation of the rôle.

In the same manner, Samson and Delilah ought to sing the duet in the second act without worrying about 'acting' it.

In the operatic repertoire there are only two works which are an exception and in which realism may be adapted to the words: *Boris* and *Pelléas*. The others have some of their roots in oratorio, in some way or the other, and it will depend on the value of the musical execution whether the public feels inclined to forget their scenic improbabilities.

The interminable debates between conformism and the spirit of reform are a special result of the obsession for 'doing it differently' from how it used to be done. Most producers of today endeavour to do the reverse of how Albert Carré did it. Conformism as it is generally understood certainly consists in preserving and increasing prejudice and error. But some traditions of the past can be a help to the future. At the Conservatoire, despite budgetary restrictions, classes have been created the usefulness of which is at least debatable. But no one thought of restoring the classes of posture and of fencing for future Romeos and Iphigénies.

Nowadays posture on the stage is deteriorating—firstly through carelessness of posture while not on stage, and then also because people no longer think of noble bearing on stage. Only a few survivors from a bygone age still worry about it at all. I sometimes watched Georges Wague, whose glorious career of mime destined him to teach production—the right kind. Concerning false ideas as represented by opera, he finds that the resultant obligations must be shouldered. Three essential precepts are the basis of his teaching:

A minimum of gesture corresponds to a maximum of expression.

Gesture is only the supplement of thought.

Without thought, gesture is useless.

He invented 'scales' and 'exercises' of plastic gesture which, he said, are as indispensable as singing exercises, and are generally neglected. Among these exercises, the increasing speed of following an event with one's eyes is a powerful factor of expression. He insists that the belief that 'it will go better in costume' is completely false. Georges Wague in plain clothes is able to give the impression of Ulysses or Faust, and even of Pénélope or Mireille, because he makes himself *be* these characters.

Once, Colette expressed the opinion that actors might gain more ease if forced in their early days to study their scenes in tights, without the help of pockets for their hands, or of cigarettes and lighters.

We have in France producers who do respect Albert Carré's memory and who are able to use his inspiration while at the same time profiting from modern achievements. For them it is essential that they should utilize any methods of interest and fuse them with their other ideas, but not set them up as principles for the only reason that they are 'interesting'. Nothing dates more quickly than yesterday's up-to-the moment method.

These are producers who will be able to save opera in France by ridding it of its abuses and of those who perpetrate them. We may apply to them Count Noüy's smiling philosophy:

> Infatuated by their cerebral faculties, these individuals believe only in what they are able to understand, viz., to translate limited experience into mechanical models. Their reasoning is that of racing greyhounds which, pursuing a hare in a real field, stop dead all of a sudden and say to each other: 'Aren't we silly, this is not a real hare—why, it hasn't even any wheels!'

XV. AT THE MICROPHONE

IT IS generally admitted that in front of the microphone the conductor is faced with new problems. His ordinary working method has to obey entirely new laws, and he must be prepared for a type of criticism or of approval the existence of which was previously unknown to him.

Clearly he cannot count upon the helpful atmosphere created by a public he felt behind him, attentive and critical, but always ready to be impressed. At the microphone, a laboratory atmosphere prevails which contains its own sometimes unpredictable and sometimes unfavourable reactions. Before the microphone, the first demand is to adopt an abstract attitude. And it is this abstract attitude which is for all interpreters and particularly for the conductor the one fundamental virtue which is most difficult to acquire and to preserve. And then also, the conductor must be diplomatic and delicate in his relations with the technical staff. The technicians are prone to go beyond the scientific limit of their collaboration and to reject out of hand any suggestion coming from a musician. I have to add that there are happy exceptions which I had the pleasure of experiencing.

As I have devoted an important portion of another work (author's *Mouvement Contraire*, vol. II) to radio, I shall here confine myself to some essential generalities.

Interpretations before the microphone have become too specialized. A famous film-star once gave a demonstration of three different interpretations of the same scene: for the theatre, for radio, and for the screen. A radio journal held a plebiscite among artists about the usefulness of establishing a radio class at the Conservatoire. It will easily be realized that all those who cast ambitious glances toward such a chair were in favour—in our age where, despite national economizing, it seems more important to create good jobs for people than to find good people for jobs.

If there are special radio interpretations, the logical consequence would be never to have a transmission of a public concert or of a theatrical performance, as these must *a priori* be inferior. Yet the public seems to like them best.

The truth is that the microphone is more pitiless than even the camera. With the latter, there are still tricks, through lighting; with the microphone, there are none whatsoever. The microphone demands that 'everything must be there'.

Before the microphone the conductor too often adopts the mentality of his musicians who 'do a recording' or 'do a broadcast', which means getting as much money as possible by spending as little time as possible.

He will seat his orchestra as the engineers demand, and he will accept the number and the position of the microphones which they advise, as 'this makes it easy for them'!

Besides, there exists a separate intermediary position between the science of wireless transmission and the art of music, that of the person in the control-room. This person, a musician, ought to be on the musicians' side, but is generally under the influence of the technicians. He may become the most formidable intermediary because the irresistible attraction of his meters causes him to modify at his pleasure the intentions of even the conductor. Seeing a *forte* approach, he 'thinks' that it may cause a 'blast', and he levels it down in advance. In the same manner, at the approach of a *piano*, he will 'think' it may not 'come over' and will increase the volume. Result: not considering that the conductor—if he is a real one—may have already adjusted his dynamics to the needs of the microphone, the man in the control-room levels them all to the indifferent *mezzoforte* flayed by Colonne.

Everything we have said in this book applies without exception to broadcasting as well as to all other sorts of performances. The conductor must not regard the microphone with the haughty contempt or indifference of those who have not yet understood the great importance of this new servant of music. But he also must not allow himself to be over-impressed by the microphone behind him. If he has talent, the microphone will surely show it; if he has none, the microphone won't give it to him.

The conductor, the only person responsible for the execution, must realize that in radio he has under his direction not only his players and his singers, but also the technicians, who must put their science at the service of music though they are sometimes inclined to reverse this relationship. Consequently, the conductor must control the collaboration of the engineers as well as that of the others. Once he has rehearsed a work to his own satisfaction, calculating the factors of wireless transmission, it is possible for him to 'listen in' to different portions of the work in the control-room. For this purpose, the conducting may be left for a few moments in the hands of the leader (concert-master) or of another conductor.

It is always necessary to watch that the loudspeaker in the control-room is regulated so as to give the correct idea of the orchestral density—a point often neglected by the engineers. In order to check up on it, the conductor must place himself at the door or at the observation window, so that he can listen with one ear to the orchestra itself and with the other to the loudspeaker.

We have said that the seating of the orchestra and chorus should not be changed for broadcasting. One sole exception must be made for the percussion section if there are special microphones for the choir. But then, microphones ought to be directed and perfected so that they 'take' only the choir. The percussion instruments, if they have to be re-seated, can find their places at one of the sides, half way up the platform, according to the dimensions of the hall. Anyway, neither percussion nor brass should ever upset the sound, except under conductors who mistake noise for strength.

Let us now discuss the system of multiple microphones, generally used for recording and broadcasting and more frequently detrimental than favourable to faithful reproduction.

The decision as to number and placing of microphones generally lies in the hands of mere engineers. For operatic transmissions I have actually seen microphones placed near off-stage music! In other words, the effect of distance was deliberately destroyed. It is the conductor's duty to oppose heresies of this kind—but he has to be pretty alert to notice them.

In studios for recording as well as for broadcasting pride of place is given to the 'singers' microphone' or 'soloists' microphone' which neither technicians nor soloists themselves dream of discarding. Placed on the conductor's left, it collects the confessions of the singers who swarm around it like bees round a honey-pot. The result for the listener is a generally thunderous and purely vocal quality against a distantly strummed orchestral background. The controller can then turn the knob for the orchestra to his heart's content. The orchestra in the studio will cease observing dynamics and accompanying discreetly. The players know what is going on in the control-room and even feel that they have nothing whatsoever to do with the singers who are strangers going their own separate ways.

The conductor is too indifferent to this ill-omened instrument, the main function of which seems to be to disrupt the context of the polyphony. In modern music the listener will be even more aware of these microphone misdeeds: the 'soloists' microphone' separates the voice entirely from its harmonic background. But in modern works the voice is unthinkable without this very background. The singing will then sound ludicrous and monotonous. In the world of the gramophone thousands are spent on advertising certain 'complete recordings' which, through the wrong balance between orchestra and singers, are a complete distortion of the composers' idea. And the composer can't defend himself.

In radio, the devastating instrument suppresses the atmosphere. No 'air' from the surrounding space can make itself felt. The necessity for this 'air' which has gradually been acknowledged since the principle of sound-absorbing studio walls has definitely been rejected. Even in dramatic transmissions the actors sound as if talking in a box, and any impression of the three dimensions of space is absent. The film-star who during her demonstration—theatre, radio, film—first yelled her part 'on stage' and then whispered it into the microphone 'for radio', simply succeeded in making it sound wrong 'for radio'.

Finally, let us say that, if only a conductor would *dare* to recommend his technicians to simplify instead of to complicate, music would gain thereby. This is our main interest. Just one microphone would be enough for orchestra and soloists —instrumentalists or singers. They should be placed just as for a concert, on the conductor's left, or slightly in front of him, and they should face the only microphone which should, one day, even become sensitive enough to 'take' the choir, too.

It is hardly necessary to say that in several years of experience I have made numerous tests, all of which corroborate the above-mentioned theories. However, radio and even the gramophone are still in their infancy, like that period of primitive motoring when you dressed in Eskimo furs and protected your eyes with stone-breakers' glasses to do twenty miles per hour. And then the mysteries of the aerial create favourable conditions for innumerable jobs. Broadcasting offices are supposed to be clean and parasite-free. Yet no one seems to fear that type which is most detrimental to progress: the one on two legs. . . .

XVI. IN MEMORIAM

HITHERTO, I have spoken mostly about living French conductors. I was also privileged to know some masters of the past generation, men who have honoured and adorned their profession.

Strangely enough, there seem to be fewer conductors of genius in France than in other countries. This parsimony of fate is perhaps responsible for the fact that certain prerogatives which are conferred upon a conductor in other countries are denied to him in France. His position is limited to that of an artistic executive.

However, it was not always so. For long years, Colonne and Lamoureux, for example, were absolute masters in their own house. They held the management of their concerts in their own hands. They engaged and paid their musicians themselves. Their term at the head of the Opéra orchestra has remained legendary. It was said that Lamoureux, mounting the rostrum for a rehearsal, used to deposit a revolver next to his score and that one night he told a flautist who had made a mistake: 'Monsieur, I want you to feel that three bullets have been fired at you!' Of course, we have to allow for exaggeration and fantasy when listening to such tales. But it cannot be denied that at that time it was not very comfortable to be an orchestral musician.

The duration of rehearsals was unlimited, and Edouard Colonne would interrupt his orchestra under some flimsy pretext at a quarter-to-twelve, turn back all the pages of his score and then announce with a honeyed voice: 'Gentlemen, once more from the beginning, please....'! But this meant the whole of *La Damnation de Faust*! And if there was a

N

grumble, Colonne would add in the same sort of voice: 'Well, it seems you don't like music?'

The rehearsals in the Cirque d'Eté were no less frightful. The absence of heating in the middle of winter forced the musicians to play wrapped in their overcoats and with their top-hats on—the professional symbol of that period—and with fingers gradually becoming stiff with cold. But Lamoureux, who never stopped his violent movements, felt almost too warm and never allowed the slightest slackening.

It has been said that these two famous pioneers often prolonged rehearsals for their own benefit, and that their indisputable leader-qualities were not sufficiently balanced by a background of musical 'humanity'. This is possible; like their predecessor Pasdeloup, Colonne and Lamoureux had come 'from the orchestra' in which they had been violinists. This was then and will always remain the best preparation for the conductor. But too often it induces him to rely only upon the professional gifts he has already, instead of adding to them that real knowledge which can only be acquired by patience. This is not the place to discuss this point, because our subject is the authority of the conductor put at the service of music. No one would ever dream of denying that Pasdeloup, Colonne and Lamoureux had as their first aim a *musical* ideal. They succeeded in putting it into reality, owing to their absolute and tenacious *authority*.

We must mention also Paul Taffanel, conductor of the *Société des Concerts du Conservatoire* and of the Opéra. He, too, dared to impose his absolute rule upon both orchestra and directors. A former member of the two orchestras he now conducted, this man with his short, bent figure and those brief, precise gestures, exercised pitiless authority. This was the period—mentioned in chapter II—when Pedro Gailhard was director. Taffanel was first conductor, and there were two others 'assisting' him. Later they were endowed by the director with 'equal' rights—but Taffanel's absolute power ceased only with his death.

Since those remote times, music has been subject to a social development which was gradually to breach the authority of the conductor. It cannot be denied that some conductors were guilty of inadmissible abuses of authority which often happened to coincide with notorious professional incompetence. The directors, of course, were of the opinion that, anyway, their very position conferred upon them some sort of universal genius. Thus, profiting by the shortcomings of some conductors, they eliminated them as professional intermediaries in their dealings with musicians and choristers. The professional musicians' and choristers' organizations were not slow in seeing the advantage if they could talk 'business' with the director in the conductor's absence. We have thus arrived at a state of affairs where I, during my forty years as conductor, was unable ever to achieve one single exception to this deplorable rule. Fear of dictatorship created a conductor-phobia which is there, all the time, and with all parties concerned. The trouble is, it breeds demagogy, the lowest form of dictatorship.

Most conductors have willingly condoned this new spirit. They veer between their superiors and their inferiors and by this opportunism they succeed in keeping their positions. After all, we now find that even certain national organizations are trying to run their business on the lines of symphony orchestra management!

Georges Marty, successor to Taffanel, was as authoritarian as Taffanel himself, at the *Société des Concerts du Conservatoire.* I was then a very young man. Marty, who was also a professor at the Conservatoire, allowed me to attend his vocal ensemble classes, and at the end of the lessons I used to accompany him to the gate. I have written about it elsewhere (author's *Diabolus in Musica*, chapter IV). Marty told me then about his first 'bust up' with the illustrious orchestra. In one of his first rehearsals, he wanted the orchestra to go through a concerto which was on the programme. The answer was that 'the soloist wasn't there'. To which he retorted that he was quite aware of this fact—only to be told that 'here, Monsieur, we never rehearse a concerto without the soloist!' We need hardly mention that Marty broke them of this custom.

A few years before, Marty had revealed his vocation as conductor at the Concerts de l'Opéra where I made my debut as orchestral player. Founded by Pedro Gailhard, the latter had entrusted the conducting of these concerts to two of his répétiteurs. One was Marty. The 'other one', however, was the favourite of the 'boss' because he came from Toulouse. Thus, he blocked his colleague all the time so that it was never possible for Marty to conduct, while the 'other one' occupied his position for about twenty years (see chapter II).

Marty revealed his mastery in one of the Concerts de l'Opéra where *La Damnation de Faust* was to be given. His colleague being unable to conduct the last rehearsals, Marty took over, galvanized the orchestra into life and gave a magnificent performance. He created the impression that he was one of the greatest French conductors—perhaps even the greatest. Of course, at the Opéra they never forgave him! Marty died prematurely. He was succeeded by Messager as head of the *Société des Concerts du Conservatoire*.

Few musicians were ever endowed like Messager with dual talents. Few conductors can have preserved so durable a reputation from their ephemeral activity. He was a composer, and he was conductor not only of the *Société des Concerts du Conservatoire* but also of the Opéra. But we always think of him as of the man who conducted the first *Pelléas* at the Opéra-Comique. We have often said so and will never get tired of repeating it. During my two terms of office as musical director of the Opéra-Comique I never *dared* to modify his tradition. Here and elsewhere I have always endeavoured to follow his example, in the hope that I might be able to restore for the listener of today the emotions he created in us.

Messager's commanding attitude, while not as fierce as Marty's or Taffanel's, was rather harsh, especially at the Opéra-Comique. At the Opéra, as everywhere else, musicians are fond of nicknaming their conductors. They called Messager 'The Pike'—obviously he cannot have been a coward!

Messager knew the rare joy of having completely satisfied Debussy, and to have filled him with confidence—Debussy, the man of genius who was so sensitive that he found it almost impossible to be present at performances of his works! Under the title *L'Enfance de Pelléas* André Messager's son published Debussy's letters to his father. They are moving and incisive; yet they contain cruel judgment on artists who are still alive and who have hitherto at least believed in the gratitude of the composer who had in any case accepted their collaboration. We are surprised at the lightheartedness with which certain publications of this sort have been undertaken. It is no less culpable to give away personal and private opinions of two people who are dead than to betray professional and confessional secrets. Even if one of the parties has consented to this posthumous publication, no one has the right to expose things which 'the other one' had written in ignorance of the fact that one day they would be put before the public.

Anxious to perpetuate the work they had done, and mindful also of the failure of the Pasdeloup venture, Colonne and Lamoureux themselves chose their successors during their lifetime and prepared them for their task. They were in the position of being able to do so and chose wisely. Times have certainly changed! The two great pioneers had probably felt that the successors they had found possessed the fundamental culture which they themselves partially lacked. Working with Colonne and Lamoureux, their protégés were thus able to acquire the necessary qualities for becoming conductors of the kind the future of French music demanded. In this manner they were able to extend their absolute authority over their musicians even after their death.

When Colonne appointed Gabriel Pierné as his assistant, the latter gave the famous orchestra an orientation which it had never known and which placed it immediately in the van of symphony orchestras. He made good his predecessor's injustices and oversights. He never interrupted his noble task of searching for new works which, carried out in a spirit of eclecticism, may still serve today as a—rarely followed— example! His appointment to Colonne's position had caused a sensation. It was to confirm the indisputable superiority of the cultured musician over the conductor 'coming from the ranks'. It was impossible to say of him, as it had been said about Colonne, that 'he had found his conductor's baton in his haversack'. Therefore he did not have that undoubted advantage of which we have spoken so often. And we have also stressed that this potential advantage will change into its opposite unless put at the service of musical sense and culture. Now it so happened that Pierné's culture and his musical understanding allowed him gradually to triumph over technical difficulties to such a point that he was able to present to us with complete perfection Debussy's masterworks—the problems of which Colonne has never been able to solve—and later those by Ravel, Schmitt, Stravinsky, and then, until his retirement, the whole production of the young French and foreign schools. If we compare his attitude with that of d'Indy, whose natural predisposition for directing orchestras was as limited as Pierné's, we find an interesting contrast of temperament. D'Indy in vain applied 'the rules' whereas Pierné developed his talent simply through his sensitivity and taste.

In one of his familiar *bons mots* Pierné defined his conductor's prerogatives as follows—and thereby proved that he was quite free from illusions: 'A concert society is a body of patrons with the conductor as its employee!' For almost a quarter of a century he gave his services unsparingly as conductor of the Concerts Colonne. This was for a person of his sensitivity a superhuman task to which he had undertaken to give the major portion of his time, at the expense of his creative work, and even of his health. Wagner himself had known in his day those discussions with orchestral committees which were necessary in order to obtain—a performance of the 'Ninth'!

Camille Chevillard, Lamoureux's son-in-law and successor, was a contemporary and co-student of Pierné's. Both of them loved music in the same manner and served it with the same integrity. But this is all they had in common. In all other respects their personalities were strikingly contrasted.

Chevillard's robust manner, his loud voice, the way in which he jeered at his musicians and at composers while rehearsing their works, were only a blind to hide his kindness and timidity. It was just like his bowler-hat which he jauntily slapped down right across his brow—just in order to prevent people from noticing his failing eyesight. His rude behaviour did not deceive anyone, and we all took him to be a benevolent bully—which was just what he was.

Musically, Chevillard did not share Pierné's catholicism. His taste had hardly developed beyond that of his father-in-law. His interpretations of the symphonies by Beethoven and Schumann were acclaimed—the latter was his favourite composer—and he conducted much Wagner and Russian music. As far as moderns were concerned, he was nervy with scores of complicated construction, and they repelled him. Often during my conversations with him, Debussy contrasted Chevillard's limitations with the fingertip-sensitivity of Pierné. I had to admit that I was aware of this.

However, Chevillard was so conscientious that he always considered it his duty to force himself to perform even those works which did not correspond to his ideal, whenever he acknowledged the composers as real musicians. Thus he succeeded in replacing Pierné's intuitive catholicism by his own catholicism of conscience which is infinitely rare and must be respected all the more.

An orchestra was founded a few years before 1900 at the Théâtre de la Porte-Saint-Martin, for the performance of a grand pantomime the music of which had been written by André Messager and Xavier Leroux. The latter was also the conductor and had surrounded himself with very young players among whom were André Caplet, Philippe Gaubert and myself. The three of us were following the double profession of composer and conductor. We fulfilled the conditions fixed by Colonne and Lamoureux when choosing two composers as their successors. Not only did the three of us come 'from the ranks', but we had also the other necessary qualifications and had found our 'field-marshal's baton' in our violin-cases. Because we were violinists—even Gaubert, who also played the flute.

The first of us ever to conduct was Caplet, who deputised sometimes for Leroux. But we were still students, and although this debut already showed his future mastery, Caplet continued his studies for the Prix de Rome as soon as the performances were over. His time as conductor was spent mostly in America. We met again later when both of us had been honoured by Debussy's friendship, at the first performance of *Le Martyre de St Sébastien*. As a conductor and as a composer Caplet was of extreme, almost morbid, sensitivity and insisted with his exceptional regard for detail on complete perfection. His supreme goal was incessantly to serve music, and he did so until his premature end.

Gaubert was just as gifted. When still a small boy he had attracted Taffanel's attention by the shape of his lips. Taffanel saw in him his successor as flautist. Those who had heard Taffanel play said that Gaubert produced the same incredible tone-quality which even the best flautists were unable to match. We might say also that quite apart from his most beautiful flute-tones Gaubert was the ideal re-incarnation of the Faun!

Taffanel marked for Gaubert from his childhood on the path which was to lead his spiritual son to the positions which he himself had occupied at the Opéra and at the *Société des Concerts du Conservatoire*. In contrast to Caplet, Gaubert was never over-much disturbed by too subtle inner controversies. The robustness of his 'manner', somewhat *al fresco*, was the opposite of Caplet's pointillism. He never spared himself, despite the warnings of his friends, conducting for twenty years at the Opéra and at the *Société des Concerts du Conservatoire*, as well as holding the chair of the conductors' and instrumentalists' classes at the Conservatoire, and adding his own fertile work as a composer. Anyway, few conductors ever did understand to what risks they exposed their talent or their health—and too often both—by taking on too many activities. In order to conduct well, one must not conduct too much. Taffanel having given his dangerous example to Gaubert, both were bound to die suddenly, when hardly on the threshold of old age.

In the happy period before the wars—in plural—Durand, the publishers, gave a series of orchestral concerts with works published by them, at the Salle Gaveau. These were conducted by Rhené-Baton, who had not figured before as a conductor. At one of the concerts we heard the first performance of Debussy's *La Mer*, which was so good that I went immediately to express my admiration to Rhené-Baton, whom I had never met.

Later, a wealthy music-lover bought from Pasdeloup's inheritors the right to launch a concert society under the name of the almost forgotten pioneer. This enterprise revolutionized musical Paris in that the orchestral musicians were not associates but were paid union rates by the directors. Rhené-Baton was entrusted with the artistic direction of the enterprise which, however, was short-lived, handicapped as it was by too high expenditure. The musicians then obtained from their director-Maecenas the permission to continue the work with their conductor under association rules.

At the Concerts Pasdeloup Rhené-Baton confirmed his remarkable mastery and conductor's gifts which were similar to Chevillard's. His exterior bearing rather pointed towards the 'spectacular' conductor by whom the public is so impressed. We have to say that he was not totally averse to taking some slight advantage of it. And then, he had a taste for travelling and went all over Europe, certainly contributing much to the decentralization of our musical life. This is how he asked first Caplet and then myself to share with him the Concerts Pasdeloup. But the association rules to which he had only conditionally consented gradually sapped his authoritarian instincts. After having several times tendered and then again withdrawn his resignation, he decided finally to resign and stuck to travelling for several years.

Towards the end of his life—shortened by a cruel disease—a strange and touching change took place. This man who had liked his public, suddenly renounced contact with it. Definitely rejecting the show-pieces of the 'guest-conductor' and the rôle which he had liked so much, he devoted his time to unknown and little-known works of the past and present which he conducted far away from the world in a broadcasting studio, for the pleasure of an invisible audience and for his own satisfaction.

Besides the great conductors we have recalled, there was a strange man who proved himself only at the age of fifty.

In one of the first orchestras in which I played I met Walter Straram, also a violinist, whose intelligence, esprit, and taste had immediately impressed me. We discovered that our fathers had been colleagues at the time when they, too, were conductors. Later we often met, playing at the same desk. Cherishing already the ambition to conduct, we often amused ourselves by trying to discover how not to conduct—by watching those who conducted us.

I lost sight of him for some years, but found him later as répétiteur at the Opéra. In between he had been to America, Bayreuth, England, speaking English and German as he played the piano—without ever having learned it—or so he said. And only at fifty was he able to put his plans into reality, thanks to a magnificent Maecenas. Henceforth being able to use the Théâtre des Champs-Elysées whenever he wanted, he selected a wonderful orchestra from among the best Parisian players and founded *his* concerts for which he was able to have an unlimited number of rehearsals.

I remember at the beginning of the Concerts Straram hearing the 'Jupiter' Symphony. It was the most beautiful performance I ever heard of this masterwork by 'Mott's Art', as Straram liked to pronounce him. But gradually, as he ventured beyond the classics, it seemed that it was not without terror that he approached the purely technical difficulties of modern scores. Musically, of course, 'Jupiter' may be more difficult to conduct than *Petrouchka*, but simply from the point of view of conducting gestures the second score presents some problems which only experience can solve, and which are not contained in the 'Jupiter'. Waiting too long until he begins to conduct, the conductor may resemble somewhat those who risk learning skiing late in life.

Perhaps also Straram's long-standing preference for Wagner —whose *Mastersingers* may even have influenced him in the choice of his christian name—prevented him from assimilating the eclecticism which he had made the guiding principle of his programmes. Some of his followers said that he was best in rehearsals, commenting on the works his musicians were playing. Very likely so. Unfortunately, the public judges conductors by their performances without their verbal comment.

This is irrelevant, and Straram deserves to be counted among those French conductors we must remember, although bad luck prevented him from showing his mettle as advantageously as the others. That wonderful 'Jupiter' performance deserves being mentioned—and then, we had so much fun together, because of all my vanished colleagues Straram knew best how to criticize with me the manners of all those conductors who couldn't conduct, and under whom we had played together.

XVII. POSTLUDE

WHILE putting all these reflections in writing, I often asked myself whether it was not futile to recall so many essential things the importance of which is so seldom recognised and admitted. I have met so many gifted beginners who did not care for perfection or even whether perfection were possible. However, it is the young ones of the sort I have mentioned who have begged me to persevere—those among whom you still find the trusting and friendly feeling of young doctors towards the 'boss': these real 'musical assistants' whom I had the great pleasure of meeting and sometimes keeping with me, who were—as Professor Gosset said—disciples, not imitators, and who freely developed their own personality—while accepting guidance.

We should have remembered one of my contemporaries as the greatest French critic but for the fact that he considered musical development finished with Fauré, Debussy, and Ravel. A fervent admirer of Anatole France, he ought to have thought like his friend, that 'the future is hidden, even from those who make it!'

It is a fact that wars, often favourable to science and medicines are disastrous to art. Certainly, music knew the 'camp-followers' of the time after the first world war, lived on turnip, after 1939, and met the profiteers of the Liberation. But it would be absurd not to count upon youth for the future of music. With the whole world influenced by the disaster of war, we should not despair of peace any more than of spring coming after winter.

We must then think of those who are on the way—they will be there! They must be guided across the ransacked gardens of the Muses. And ransacked those gardens were indeed, without mercy, in the quarter of a century after that happy period when French music had shone forth upon the world. Those who first tangled Mélisande's hair and then cut it short have replaced—as Albert Carré said—Pelléas's forest by a kitchen-garden. The age of the petrol pump was bound to be deadly to trees. But the trees will be again 'in verdure clad'.

Finally I was to find strange encouragement in this exhortation in Georges Duhamel's preface to Professor Gosset's book:

> There are some people who should concentrate the essence of their personal experience in a book. They should not leave to any-one else the task of expressing—when it is too late—what they thought of their predecessors, of their disciples, of their colleagues, of the ordeals they had to suffer, of the gifts they received from nature, and of the world at whose bosom they live and complete their destiny.

It is better to express our own thoughts badly ourselves than to leave it to someone else to taint them with his fantasy!

Marseilles 1942—Paris 1949.

APPENDIX
THE WORKS OF D. E. INGHELBRECHT

1902 DEUX ESQUISSES ANTIQUES: (a) flute and harp; (b) small orchestra.

1903 DEUX ESQUISSES: (a) piano; (b) orchestra.

1905 POEME SYLVESTRE: wind instruments.

1905 AUTOMNE. Symphonic sketches: (a) orchestra; (b) transcription for piano.

1905 PAR DELA LES FLEUVES TARIS: voice and piano.

1905 MELODIES SUR DES POESIES RUSSES: voice and piano.

1905 NOCTURNE: (a) 'cello and piano; (b) 'cello and orchestra.

1905 LA NURSERY (24 children's pieces) 5 books: (a) piano duet; (b) piano solo; (c) small orchestra.

1905 PRELUDE ET SALTARELLE: alto and piano.

1908 LA NUIT VENITIENNE (after Alfred de Musset): Musical play in three scenes.

1908 POUR LE JOUR DE LA PREMIERE NIEGE AU VIEUX JAPON: (a) orchestra; (b) transcription for piano duet.

1908 SUITE PETITE RUSSIENNE: piano solo.

1910 RAPSODIE DE PRINTEMPS: (a) orchestra; (b) transcription for piano duet.

1910 AU JARDIN DE L'INFANTE: voice and piano.

1912 LES DOMINOS of Couperin: small orchestra.

1915 QUATRE CHANSONS POPULAIRES FRANCAISES: (a) mixed choir; (b) voice and piano; (c) voice and orchestra; (d) vocal duet and piano.

1917 QUINTETTE EN UT MINEUR: (a) 2 violins, alto, 'cello and harp; (b) transcription for piano duet.

1917 IBERIA, Albeniz (Book I): orchestra.

1918 SONATINE: flute and harp or piano.

1918 PAYSAGES: piano solo.

1919 LE CANTIQUES DES CREATURES, (St Francis of Assisi): (a) mixed choir and orchestra; (b) transcription for choir and piano—solo and duet.

1920 EL GRECO. Symphonic evocations: (a) orchestra; (b) transcription for piano solo.

1921 IBERIA, Albeniz (Book III): orchestra.

1922 LE DIABLE DANS LE BEFFROI, ballet: (a) orchestra; (b) piano transcription.

1922 IMPROMPTU: alto and piano.

1923 TROIS POEMES DANSES: (a) orchestra; (b) transcription for piano solo.

1927 THEME ET VARIATIONS, from G. Fauré: orchestra.

1927 RAYON DE LUNE, ballet based on the preceding work.

1928 LA METAMORPHOSE D'EVE: (a) small orchestra; (b) transcription for piano solo.

1929 VOCALISE-ETUDE: voice and piano.

1929 SIX DANSES SUEDOISES: (a) orchestra; (b) piano solo.

1930 SINFONIA BREVE: small orchestra.

1930 PRELUDE ET FUGUE EN UT MINEUR after Bach: orchestra.

1932 LA LEGENDE DU GRAND SAINT-NICOLAS: (a) voice and small orchestra; (b) voice and piano.

1932 DERNIERES NURSERIES (6 children's pieces): (a) piano duet; (b) piano solo; (c) small orchestra.

1932 QUATRE FANFARES: brass instruments.

1936 CARNAVAL ROMANTIQUE (in collaboration with J. Variot).

1937 ENFANTINES, from Moussorgsky: voice and orchestra.

1937 LA VALSE RETROUVEE: orchestra.

1937 LA METAMORPHOSE D'EVE, ballet in one act and eight scenes: (a) orchestra; (b) transcription for piano solo.

1908 }
1937 } SCENES D'ENFANTS, from Schumann: orchestra.

1938 LA MARSEILLAISE DEPUIS ROUGET DE L'ISLE (in collaboration with René Fauchois).

1939 LE LIVRE D'OR, theme and variations: orchestra.

1939 LE REBUBLIQUE NOUS APPELLE (in collaboration with André Obey).

1939 BALLADE DANS LE GOUT IRLANDAIS: harp and orchestra.

1941 NOEL DES ENFANTS QUI N'ONT PLUS DE MAISONS of Debussy: orchestra.

1941 REQUIEM: solo voices, choir, organ and orchestra.

1943 TANT QUE NOEL DURERA: recitative, solo voices, choirs and orchestra.

1943 PASTOURELLES SUR DES NOELS ANCIENS: orchestra.

1943 DEUX NOELS: mixed choir.

1946 CHANTONS JEUNESSE (poems by Germaine Inghelbrecht): 10 small choirs of three equal voices.

1946 CHANSONS TENDRES: voice and piano, with a second voice optional.

1946 MOWGLI, after 'The Jungle Book' by Rudyard Kipling: recitative, baritone solo, choirs and orchestra.

1947 VIRAGE SUR L'AILE (libretto by Jean Magnin): operetta in 3 acts.

1948 IBERIANA: rhapsody for violin and orchestra.

1950 SONATE: piano and violin.